MY DEFENSE

Responding to Charges that
I Fully Affirm LGBTQ+ People

THOMAS JAY OORD

SacraSagePress.com

© 2024 SacraSage Press and Thomas Jay Oord

SacraSage Press, Grasmere, ID, USA

Book Interior Design: Nicole Sturk
Cover Design: Alexa M. Oord

Paperback Print: 978-1-958670-46-0
Electronic: 978-1-958670-47-7

Printed in the United States of America

Library of Congress Cataloguing-in-Publication Data
My Defense: Responding to Charges that I Fully Affirm LGBTQ+ People /
Thomas Jay Oord

Dedicated to Queer People and their Allies

TABLE OF CONTENTS

PREFACE

I changed my mind about "homosexuality" in 1994.
What many now call "LGBTQ+" or "queer" people and issues were in the 1990s usually subsumed under the single word "homosexuality." Questions about gender and sexuality were emerging in unprecedented ways in popular culture at that time. Those questions were rarely discussed in the Church of the Nazarene, however, the holiness group into which I was ordained a few years earlier (1992). To my knowledge, the issues were *never* discussed in denominational forums, except in condemnation.[1]

In a Nazarene Theological Seminary course on religious education (taught by the beloved professor Ed Robinson), two classmates and I decided to tackle "the homosexual question." Those classmates: Dana Hicks and Reg Watson. We used the Wesleyan quadrilateral to frame our exploration, a conceptual tool that uses scripture, reason, experience, and tradition to address issues.

---

1. One important exception was Kenneth Grider, a professor formerly at Nazarene Theological Seminary. For a helpful summary of Grider's views, see Michael Lodahl's essay on him in *Why the Church of the Nazarene Should be Fully LGBTQ+ Affirming* (Grasmere, Id.: SacraSage, 2023).

As I read the scholarship on the 6-8 biblical passages use to "clobber" queer people, I realized they did not apply to most queer issues in the modern world. Those who claim the Bible opposes homosexuality were also ignoring key texts about diverse sexual identities and expressions. The Bible was not as clear as I had been led to believe.

I began to wonder what principle I should use to interpret the Bible, particularly passages related to queer concerns. After all, almost no one thinks *every* Scripture verse applies today. Even those who do privilege some passages and downplay others. Few people, for instance, worry about wearing clothing of the same fabric, although there's a passage that forbids such attire. Few people think being left-handed is wrong, but there's a passage condemning it.

Furthermore, some practices considered essential earlier in history came to be thought nonessential. Take circumcision, for instance. Numerous biblical passages support circumcision as a nonnegotiable for God's people. But the church eventually decided it was not required for Christians. And several biblical passages reject women leadership in the church. But a growing number of Christians, especially in the Church of the Nazarene, think those biblical passages do not apply today. Still other passages reflected the patriarchal assumptions of the authors, assumptions we rightly reject today.

A question arose: What interpretive principle—"hermeneutic"—should I use to make sense of the Bible?

The Wesleyan theological tradition provided an interpretive principle, and I used it then and still use it now: love. When interpreting the many voices of scripture, love should be my guide. More specifically, love ought to be the lens through which I thought about sexual matters. Love is central to Jesus' life and teachings, and I think it's the major theme of the Bible.

I had an idea of what "love" meant, but it took a few years to come to a robust definition. I came to believe that to love is to act intentionally, in relational response to God and others, to promote overall well-being. To love like Jesus, we should seek the flourishing of all, especially the marginalized, poor, and vulnerable. Love does good.

Hicks, Watson, and I wrote a massive paper for Robinson's seminary class back in 1994. We argued that the Bible, as a whole, is not opposed to loving same-sex intimacy. "Homosexuality" can be healthy, we said. The experiences of many queer people points to positive elements in queer identity, orientation, and behavior. The only strong element in the quadrilateral against queer issues and people was Christian tradition. But we found research that even questioned whether the tradition consistently opposed same-sex attraction and behavior.

Having realized I should be what we today call "affirming," I faced another question: Could I stay in the Church of the Nazarene?

I like the basic theology of the Church of the Nazarene. I have deep history in the denomination, including numerous friendships and a network of relationships. I also thought a Wesleyan theology of love supports an affirming position on LGBTQ+ matters. I still think that.

Back in the 1990s, however, the Church of the Nazarene was a *long* way from becoming an affirming denomination.

I thought it might become so in my lifetime. So... should I stay or should I go?

After pondering the options, I decided I'd stay... and work for change. I committed myself to entering private conversations to promote queer affirmation and create safe places for queer people.

I knew this approach would likely mean my sometimes feeling like a "sell-out," because I couldn't be as vocal as I would like. I also knew that change is more likely when insiders act. Although the road is rocky, it's a noble task to seek change from within.

In addition to Hicks and Watson, I also discovered many other Nazarenes who thought like me about queer issues. I began to believe we could encourage change for younger Nazarenes and others who would come after us. Perhaps we would grow in numbers.

For decades, I carefully curated my conversations about queer matters. I helped queer students and functioned as a covert ally. I know many other professors, clergy, and laity who did and currently do the same. We felt good about those we helped but guilty we weren't doing more. We wished we could be more overt.

In the years that followed, my daughters matured to a stage that required my wife and I to talk with them about sexual matters—straight and gay. In our family, we were pretty open about sex in general. In fact, this openness has become a bit of an inside joke: Dad brings up sex issues at the dinner table!

A turning point in our conversations about queer issues was a family viewing of the documentary, "The Bible

Tells Me So." My older daughters knew their parents were affirming, although I don't remember using the word "affirming" then. Today, my wife and I find ourselves learning from our three daughters about queer matters, language, and etiquette. The educational tables have turned!

Another important series of events in 2015 involved my being laid off from Northwest Nazarene University. Officially, I was laid off due to low enrollment; I was *not* laid off for my views on queer matters. The real reason for my layoff was that the President and influential leaders outside the university thought I was too progressive on matters related to open and relational theology, evolution, and other "divisive topics."

Being forced out of the university was painful. In fact, I consider it evil what was done to me and others. I will always be grateful to colleagues, students, community members, friends, and family for their support through the ordeal. It was a rough ride, and we have scars!

I believe God "squeezed" some good from the evil done, however. No longer associated with the university, I had greater freedom to speak openly about queer matters. I could support queer students and friends more overtly. And I could advocate openly for change in the denomination by explaining why the Church of the Nazarene ought to become fully affirming.

In late 2021, a group of people associated with the Holiness Partnership sent accusations against me to my district superintendent. Some accusations were theologically oriented, but they were naïve or baseless. The group rightly accused me of being LGBTQ+ affirming, however.

The district superintendent's decision to take those accusations seriously started a series of painful events.

The documents in this book were written in response to those events. They include…

1) a document I wrote for a 2024 trial in which I was charged with teaching against doctrine. Because I openly called for change, I was also charged with acting in ways unbecoming a minister. As of this writing, the trial should occur in the summer of 2024.

2) a document I wrote for a February 2022 hearing at which I defended myself. As part of that defense, I said the Church of the Nazarene should become fully LGBTQ+ affirming. Hearing committee members recommended that I *not* be disciplined. But the district superintendent took away my assignment and soon thereafter forbade me to preach.

3) the publication of 90+ essays as a book I co-edited with my daughter Alexa called *Why the Church of the Nazarene Should Become Fully LGBTQ+ Affirming*.

4) other documents of related interest, including a blog essay calling my critics "disingenuous" for criticizing my calls for change while seeking changes themselves and support from the local congregation I attended.

I will resist the urge to summarize here the pages of this book. I encourage you to read the material. I offer these documents for several reasons, not the least of which I think they can help establish love at the center of how the Church of the Nazarene responds to queer people and LGBTQ+ issues.

A lot has changed in the 30 years since I changed my mind about queer issues. But my ultimate aim remains the same: to love. These documents are expressions of that aim, and I hope you find them inspiring and useful.

THOMAS JAY OORD

MY RESPONSE TO BILL OF CHARGES

CHARGES:

This document is my response to a Bill of Charges given to me in early August, 2023 by Church of the Nazarene Intermountain District Superintendent Scott Shaw and signed by Rev. Mike Seward and Rev. Libby Gerdes. The opening paragraph of the charges says:

> Rev. Thomas J. Oord, who is a member of the clergy of the Church of the Nazarene, is being charged with both (a) of conduct unbecoming a minister and (b) of teaching doctrines out of harmony with the doctrinal statements of the Church of the Nazarene, in violation of Section 606 of the *Manual* of the Church of the Nazarene ("*Manual*"). This Bill of Charges is submitted in accordance with the *Manual*, and the Rules of Procedure of the Church of the Nazarene ("Rules"), including but not limited to Rule 1406.

The remainder of the document given to me offers alleged evidence for these charges. I am unaware of any previous communication on LGBTQ+ issues with either Gerdes or Seward; consequently, I suspect most of this evidence derives from or is filtered through District Superintendent Shaw. The fact that Gerdes and Seward have signed charges against me without dialoguing with me is contrary to *Manual* paragraph 603.1, which says, "Individuals in conflict should approach one another in humility with hope of reconciliation."

In what follows, I offer detailed responses to these charges. More importantly, I provide an overall defense of my approach to God, love, faith, and sexuality. The fundamental issue at stake in this trial is whether the Church of the Nazarene will love queer people by affirming their identities, orientation, and healthy sexual behaviors.

My Pleas:

The love of Christ compels me to accept and affirm queer people (2 Cor. 5:14). The Bill of Charges reveals, however, that some people oppose my attempts to express *agape* love toward some of the most vulnerable and rejected.

Love compels me to embrace queer people and their healthy sexual behaviors, identities, and orientations. Love prompts me to urge denominational leaders and laity to engage in genuine conversation with queer people and their allies. Love compels me to work for changes to the denomination's stance on human sexuality.

The *Manual* statement on human sexuality in the Covenant of Christian Conduct does *not* reflect love well. It does not give witness to the abundant life queer people enjoy as they cooperate with the Spirit. The statement creates obstacles for allies and clergy who love queer people and who seek to include them fully in the life of the church. The statement on human sexuality is not the loving witness it should be, and it must change if the denomination is to fulfill its call to promote holiness.

Love should compel us to celebrate healthy nonheteronormative sexual behavior, identities, attractions, and orientations.

- To the charge of "conduct unbecoming a minister," I plead *not guilty*.

I have *not* acted in ways unbecoming of a minister. I have sought to live a life of love. I will show that each claim in the Bill of Charges is based either on 1) misleading statements by those who accuse me, 2) misunderstandings of my behavior, or 3) unintentional errors.

The phrase "conduct unbecoming a minister" is typically used to describe moral failures, such as adultery. I have not committed such moral failures. My attempts to live a life of love are not morally unbecoming, even when they sometimes brought strong objections from critics and made life difficult for District Superintendent Shaw as he dealt with those critics. Living a life of love—even when doing so prompts disagreement—is not conduct unbecoming of a minister.

- To the charge of "teaching doctrines out of harmony with the doctrinal statements of the Church of the Nazarene," I plead *not guilty*.

The *Manual* does not consider the Covenant of Christian Conduct to be doctrine. Consequently, the charge that I am teaching doctrines out of harmony with doctrinal statements is mistaken. Despite what some have claimed, the statement on human sexuality is *not* an essential doctrine of faith.

- Were I to be charged with working to change the Covenant of Christian Conduct to better reflect the love revealed in Jesus, I would plead... *guilty of loving LGBTQ+ people and encouraging the Church of the Nazarene to do the same.*

For years, I have stated my intentions to encourage changes to the statement on human sexuality in the Covenant of Christian Conduct. My actions have not transgressed any *Manual* statements about how to encourage this change. My actions align with the denomination's ongoing efforts to reflect holiness theology when responding to the Spirit.

To fulfill its holy calling, the Church of the Nazarene must become LGBTQ+ affirming.

HISTORICAL BACKGROUND

I was raised in the Church of the Nazarene. For me, that meant being dedicated as an infant and attending faithfully a local Nazarene congregation (Othello, WA). It meant attending Nazarene church camps, Nazarene quizzing, Nazarene basketball tournaments, Nazarene conventions, Nazarene discipleship retreats, Nazarene talent competitions, Nazarene music events, Nazarene mission trips, and more.

For my education, I studied at Northwest Nazarene (College) University (Nampa, ID) and graduated with a degree in religion. After serving as a full-time youth pastor in a Nazarene congregation (Walla Walla, WA), I studied holiness theology at Nazarene Theological Seminary (KC, MO). I graduated with honors, learned from leading theologians in the denomination, and earned a Master of Divinity. I earned another Master's degree and a Ph.D. in religion at Claremont Graduate University (Claremont, CA). While earning these degrees, I worked as a pastor in a Nazarene congregation (Bloomington, CA).

During my professorial years at Nazarene institutions, I played a significant role in the founding of the Early Church service at Nampa First Church of the Nazarene and the planting of The Table Church of the Nazarene (Nampa, ID). Both grew significantly. I served most recently in pastoral ministry at Real Life Community Church of the Nazarene (Nampa, ID).

I have taught theology, philosophy, and ministry classes for more than twenty years, ministering as a professor at

Eastern Nazarene College (Quincy, MA) and Northwest Nazarene University (Nampa, ID). I've lectured at almost every U.S. college, university, or seminary sponsored by the denomination and lectured at Nazarene churches, retreats, and educational institutions on six continents. I've written or edited over thirty books, including four with Nazarene Publishing House and several on holiness. I now direct a doctoral program in theology at Northwind Theological Seminary (FL), with students around the world.

I recite my history, education, pastoral ministry, and positions to make this point: It is *because of* holiness theology, not in spite of it, that I am LGBTQ+ affirming.

My experience in the Church of the Nazarene and my learning from its greatest minds compel me to advocate for the full inclusion of queer people. The overall themes of scripture lead me to be an ally. Like most scholars, I know that biblical passages cited to reject queer people are better understood in light of biblical themes of love. To love LGBTQ+ people is to embrace them in their queerness and to affirm their healthy sexual expressions.

The denomination's doctrinal statements—especially related to sanctification—*compel* me to change the *Manual's* statement on sexuality. This is a matter of theological consistency. The present statement contradicts the ways of love stated or implied in the Articles of Faith and elsewhere in the *Manual*. While my goal to include queer people derives primarily from love, I would like the *Manual* to reflect a coherent and biblically oriented theology of holiness.

In short, my desire to see the statement on human sexuality changed arises from what is good in the theology, discipleship, and warm-hearted piety of the Church of the Nazarene. I am not bringing alien ideas to bear nor coming to this discussion misinformed. Few people in the denomination can match my theological training, speaking, and publishing on theology, holiness, and love.

My love for LGBTQ+ people reflects the *best* in Wesleyan-Holiness theology.

What Does it Mean to Love Queer People?

Living a life of love is my primary purpose. It's the center of what it means to follow Jesus and be in Christian community. With Jesus and the writers of scripture, I think love matters most. With John Wesley, I believe love is the heart of holiness. Nazarenes who embrace queer people often claim, like I do, that love motivates them to be fully LGBTQ+ affirming.

When I talk to those who *do not* fully affirm queer people, I rarely hear them appeal to love. Most non-affirming people employ a particular way of interpreting biblical passages they think applies to contemporary queer issues. This interpretation justifies, in their minds, opposition to queer behaviors, identities, and issues. A few will also appeal to the historical church when opposing LGBTQ+ people and issues.

Some who embrace the current *Manual* statement on human sexuality *claim* to love queer people. They say they "love the sinner, but hate the sin," which means they think same-sex behavior or nonheteronormative identity is sinful. Their opposition to queer people is, as they put it, "for their own good."

I appreciate the claim that love seeks what's good. After all, to love is to act intentionally, in relational response to God and others, to promote overall well-being. Love aims for flourishing. But the claim to want what is good for queer people while simultaneously opposing their healthy sexual behaviors, orientation, and identities makes no sense. It is *not* loving.

The Bible does not support well the non-affirming view. Biblical scholars have addressed these issues in books and articles. (See bibliography among the appendices.) But I want to mention other problems with claiming to love queer people while opposing them and their allies.

First, people who love well *listen*. Loving queer people means taking their queer testimonies into account when discerning what love asks of us. True listening means affording dignity to those who speak and being open to changing one's mind. The vast majority of LGBTQ+ people insist that to love them well means to affirm their identities, orientations, and healthy sexual behavior. Those who claim to love queer people while ignoring what queer people say are not loving well. They're not listening.

Second, love seeks well-being. It seeks what Jesus called "abundant life" and biblical writers call "blessedness," "*shalom,*" or "eternal life." The overwhelming scientific consensus is that queer people can experience well-being while embracing their queer identities and orientations. According to Appendix paragraph 923 in the *Manual,*

Nazarenes are supposed to be "open to scientific explanations…," but according to the scientific consensus, same-sex sexual behavior can be healthy. Committed same-sex relationships can promote blessedness, wholeness, and flourishing.

Third, I find that most non-affirming people do not have close relationships with queer people. They don't know well those whose "lifestyle" they don't affirm. John Wesley was right to argue that it's difficult to love well those about whom we know little. Many are also misinformed, and some are fed misinformation by religious leaders.

While non-affirming folk *think* they love, queer people don't experience them as loving.

HEALTHY SEXUALITY

The identities, orientations, and sexual behavior of LGBTQ+ people can be healthy. I say "can be" not "is always" healthy, because I'm not saying queer people are morally perfect. But heteronormative people are also not perfect. At stake, of course, is what it means for sex and sexuality to be "healthy."

In broad terms, "healthy" pertains to activities that promote well-being in various ways. Healthy sexual identities, orientations, and behaviors promote what's good, beneficial, or flourishing. Healthy sexuality enhances us psychologically, socially, and physically. Healthy same-sex sexual behavior can include the romance, pleasure, and intimacy sometimes found in healthy opposite-sex sexual behavior.[1] I advocate for sexual healthiness within the context of a committed relationship or (when possible) marriage.

I know LGBTQ+ people who experience the sanctification described in Article 10 of the *Manual*. They are sanctified. They have been transformed "into the likeness of Christ," are "made free from original sin, or depravity," have been "brought into a state of entire devotement to God," express "the holy obedience of love made perfect," enjoy the "infilling of the Holy Spirit," experience "cleansing from sin," are "empowered for life and service," "grow in grace as a Christlike disciple," improve "in Christlikeness of character and personality," are "participating in the means of grace, especially the fellowship, disciplines, and sacraments of the Church," and grow in "grace and in wholehearted love to God and neighbor."

Unhealthy sexuality is manipulative, non-consensual, and harmful to bodies and relationships. Rape, bestiality, and pedophilia are unhealthy. Such sexuality hurts, isolates, leads to pain, and strains relationships. But "queer" is not the same as "unhealthy." Both straight and queer people can engage in healthy or unhealthy sexual behavior.

Healthy queer sexual relationships promote a high quality of life.

The condemnation of LGBTQ+ people causes them great harm. Conversion therapy, for instance, rarely if ever

---

1. In some respects, same-sex partnerships are *healthier*, on average, than traditional ones. See the Gottman study on same-sex relationships: https://www.gottman.com/about/research/same-sex-couples/#:~:text=Results%20from%20the%20Gottman%20Gay,in%20how%20they%20receive%20it

helps, and it most often hurts. Queer people face excessive violence. Sometimes this treatment leads homophobes to kill queer people; other times, it leads queer people to take their own lives. Queer people are far less likely to attempt suicide if the communities in which they live accept them.[2]

LGBTQ+ people are also more susceptible to mental health problems because of the social, emotional, and religious condemnation they face. One study shows that when families reject their LGBTQ children, those children are 8.4 times more likely to attempt suicide, 5.9 times more likely to have high levels of depression, and 3.4 times more likely to use illegal drugs than LGBTQ children with supportive families.[3]

The Church of the Nazarene's statement on human sexuality does not help queer people. It can easily justify their mistreatment. When the church does not embrace queer identities, orientation, and healthy sexual behavior, abusers believe violence against queer people is warranted. The *Manual* statement on human sexuality supports homophobia.

Rather than help, the statement on human sexuality hurts LGBTQ+ people.

I believe Jesus loves queer people and celebrates their healthy sexual expressions. I also believe Jesus would seek

---

2. See "The Trevor Project: 2022 National Survey on LGBTQ Youth Mental Health," https://www.thetrevorproject.org/survey-2022/

3. See "Parents' rejection of a child's sexual orientation fuels mental health problems," March 2009, Vol 40, No. 3 Online: https://www.apa.org/monitor/2009/03/orientation

changes to the denomination's Covenant of Christian Conduct. He would speak out, boldly calling for repentance, standing for the marginalized. Jesus would do so even if it made his critics angry and brought discomfort to his district superintendent.

This means that, in our context, Jesus would likely be given a Bill of Charges and brought to trial in the Church of the Nazarene. Like me, Jesus would be considered "divisive" and charged with "promoting an agenda contrary" to the denomination. Accusers would say he "taught and promoted ideas, beliefs, and doctrine out of harmony with" the denomination's view of human sexuality.

Ironically, Jesus would not be welcome in a group that bears his name.

Addressing the Alleged Evidence Against Me

It did not surprise me when District Superintendent Shaw gave me the Bill of Charges signed by Seward and Gerdes. I suspected opponents to my love for queer people would want to silence me. But it surprised me to find they charged me with "conduct unbecoming a minister."

I have done nothing immoral in my efforts to love queer people. My "crime" is urging the Church of the Nazarene to change its statement on human sexuality. I would like the denomination to reflect God's love for all. Love motivates my conduct.

If love is "conduct unbecoming a minister," no one should be a minister.

Sometimes, of course, attempts to love are misunderstood. Sometimes a lover's actions are misinterpreted or misconstrued. And sometimes lovers make honest mistakes. As I read the alleged evidence to support the claim I have engaged in conduct unbecoming a minister, I find it lands in three broad categories: 1) misleading statements by those who accuse me, 2) misinterpretations of my behavior, or 3) unintentional errors on my part.

None of the evidence supports the "conduct unbecoming a minister" claim.

Mike Seward and Libby Gerdes signed the Bill of Charges. To my knowledge, I have not had direct or written communication with either Seward or Gerdes on these matters. Given my conversations with District Superintendent Shaw, however, I assume he played the primary role in formulating the Bill of Charges and gathering evidence. Consequently, I suspect most misleading statements and misinterpretations come from Shaw. Perhaps if Seward and Gerdes had approached me directly about the alleged evidence, which the *Manual* requires them to do, they would not have signed the charges.

In what follows, I address each charge. I show why none supports the claim I have engaged in conduct unbecoming a minister. I am not guilty.

1. "Published false and misleading statements to third parties in an email." Specifically, on March 22, 2022, Rev. Oord made false and misleading statements as to the outcome of his meeting with District Superintendent Shaw and published those false and

misleading statements to third parties in an email (see below timeline).

My Response: This charge, itself, is false and misleading.

First, to say I "published" the note in question is false. To "publish" something is to make it available to the public. To say I sent the note to "friends and supporters" is also misleading. I did not post the message on social media, put it in an article, send it to the media, or circulate it in a group email. It is a brief, hurriedly written, private note to one of my advisors.

According to Shaw, the advisor to whom I sent this private note mentioned its contents to someone else. That person then contacted Shaw. Shaw thought the note indicated he agreed with my LGBTQ+ view. It does not say this. When Shaw asked me to send the note, I complied promptly. I had nothing to hide. The note was a brief, private, and hurried message not meant for public consumption.

Second, it is misleading to say I wrote the note about "the outcome of (my) meeting with District Superintendent Shaw." The note did not characterize my meeting with Shaw alone. Its contents describe my impression of a District Advisory Board meeting, and that impression was based upon conversations with Shaw *and* two advisory board members. Those two came to me (I did not seek them out) following the DAB meeting discussing my case. Their portrayal of the DAB meeting differed somewhat from Shaw's.

When Shaw said he thought my note misrepresented him, I disagreed. But to placate him, I offered to send a revised note to my advisors to clarify that Shaw did not agree with my views. But Shaw did not want me to send a follow-up. This suggested that clarity and accuracy were not his primary aims.

Shaw then disciplined me. He took away my assignment at Real Life Community Church of the Nazarene. For writing a private note to an advisor that he misinterpreted, Shaw unilaterally took my assignment. And he did so without following due process for disciplinary action.

Shaw considers my writing the note in question conduct unbecoming a minister. We know this, because he lists it in the evidence for the present trial. Shaw calls what I did "inappropriate steps to promoting information that is in conflict with the Covenant of Christian Conduct" and that I "misrepresented both (Shaw's) position and that of the District Advisory board." But Shaw's disciplinary action to remove my assignment contradicts what the *Manual* requires. He did not follow due process, which involves written accusations, an investigation committee, official charges, and so on.

Shaw's discipline put me on the *Manual's* clock toward losing my credentials. Paragraph 539.1 says, "A member of the clergy ... unassigned for four or more consecutive years is considered to be no longer participating as a member of the clergy and is required to file his or her credential." Despite an investigative committee and District Advisory Board not recommending that I be disciplined, Shaw put me on the clock to lose my credentials.

By submitting this note/incident as evidence for the present trial, Shaw is now caught in a bind. He's claiming my private note is evidence I acted unbecoming a minister. But he can't say this *and* say that he followed due process. He can't have it both ways.

Let me explain:

1. If the note *is* evidence I acted in an unbecoming manner, Shaw should have convened an investigative committee in the Spring of 2022. But he ignored due process.

2. If the note is *not* evidence I acted in an unbecoming manner, Shaw wrongly disciplined me. He unassigned me and started the clock to forfeit my credentials.

I believe the private note is *not* evidence I acted in a manner unbecoming a minister. If those hearing my case think otherwise, they should know that Shaw has already disciplined me for the note. I cannot be disciplined a second time for the same "crime."

In sum, I did not *publish* the note in question. Its contents are not false nor misleading, and they reflect more than Shaw's impression of the DAB meeting. When I offered to write a clarifying note, Shaw did not want me to do so. And Shaw cannot both offer this note as evidence of conduct unbecoming a minister and justify his failure to use due process when he put me on the path to losing my credentials.

2. "Misrepresented the nature and outcome of the DAB's meeting and decisions." Specifically, on April 5, 2023, and May 25, 2023, Rev. Oord made public false and misleading statements which misrepresented the nature and outcome of the District Advisory Board's (DAB) meeting and decisions on his accusations and investigation (see below timeline).

My Response: This charge arises from unintentional errors and the work of internet trolls.

To explain my response to this charge, I should start at the beginning. A list of accusations against me was sent to District Superintendent Shaw in late 2021. Those accusations came from elders outside the Intermountain District, most with connections to the Holiness Partnership.

Shaw met with me and asked if I wanted to defend myself or turn in my credentials. After talking with my wife Cheryl, I chose to defend myself. Those accusations then became the center of an investigative hearing that the Intermountain District office organized and for which I wrote a defense. (See my defense document among the appendices.)

The hearing took place in February 2022 and had all the markings of a trial. I sent my defense document to the committee beforehand. Then, for several hours, I verbally defended myself and responded to questions. In my writing and oral comments, I clearly stated that the denomination's statement on human sexuality needed changing. I said I intended to help bring about that change. I'm grateful to Pastor Sarah Riley, who served as my council during this interrogation.

In response, the investigative committee sent a recommendation to the District Advisory Board. They recommended that I *not* be disciplined, despite my explicit rejection of the *Manual's* statement on human sexuality. The District Advisory Board subsequently discussed the committee's recommendation. Failing to have the support needed for disciplinary action, the process did not proceed.

In my attempts thereafter to describe what had transpired, I occasionally said that I endured a "trial." I sometimes said the "charges" leveled against me did not result in discipline. I did not realize I should have said I endured an "investigative hearing" rather than a "trial" and that I faced "accusations" instead of "charges." My failure to use precise language was unintentional. I suspect few people would know the correct language for this process, however, given that what was happening is rare in the Church of the Nazarene. And the *Manual* is not clear on these matters.

Nearly a year later, District Superintendent Shaw alerted me to my misleading language. He said I should describe what had transpired as an "investigative hearing" instead of a "trial" and talking about "accusations" instead of "charges." He reminded me that two people could decide to sign a Bill of Charges against me, because it remained open.

At the time, I thought using precise language was inconsequential and Shaw was making a mountain out of a molehill. He was quibbling over semantics. Nevertheless,

I tried to use the language Shaw wanted thereafter, especially when talking to Nazarenes.

In the spring of 2023, I realized why Shaw cared about my language. The podcast evidence in the Bill of Charges points to moments I accidentally used imprecise language. Nazarenes did not host these podcasts, they were not aimed at Nazarene audiences, and I suspect few if any Nazarenes listen regularly. But Shaw began receiving complaints based on them.

Shaw tells me he was not listening to the podcasts cited as evidence. I believe him. How did Shaw come to know about my mistakes? I suspected the answer was that my critics were searching for evidence and then sending it to the district office. Shaw has since confirmed this.

For more than 20 years, I have been pestered by critics who want me disciplined, silenced, fired, or ushered out of the denomination. People and groups like Reformed Nazarene, Concerned Nazarenes, and the Holiness Partnership make my life difficult. These self-appointed "defenders of the faith" stalk me. It's tiring. They search the internet and social media for evidence to send those in authority over me. They've influenced my past employers and District Superintendent Shaw. (See my 2023 response, "Disingenuous," among the appendices.)

People who engage in bad faith or search for gotcha statements on social media are called "internet trolls." Trolls have bad motives, take statements out of context, cause problems where there are none, and use uncharitable tactics. They don't want sincere conversation; they're hunting for damning evidence. To take trolls seriously is to "feed" them. Some alleged evidence offered in the Bill of Charges reveals that Shaw, unfortunately, does not always ignore the trolls. Their pestering has led Shaw to admit fatigue.

I have many times expressed empathy for what District Superintendent Shaw endures. I know my critics hound and harass him. Because of what the trolls have done to me, I knew from the outset my efforts to see the *Manual* changed would bring Shaw suffering. I felt bad about this. This is what I meant when I said my actions would be a "thorn in his side." Of course, I have also suffered greatly for taking the stand that I do. For me, it's *more* than a thorn. But I consider the pain Shaw and I endure to pale in significance to the pain queer people suffer.

In sum, I admit to accidentally using imprecise language. My errors do not amount to moral failures, however. Unless one thinks ministers must be mistake-free, my conduct has not been unbecoming.

3. "Worked outside agreed upon procedures and processes...to invoke change in the church." Specifically, on various dates, Rev. Oord has worked outside of the agreed upon procedures and processes of the Church of the Nazarene in an attempt to invoke change in the church regarding his opinions (*Manual* 25.8, 305.8, 912 Rule 14-16).

My response: This charge is false.

The Bill of Charges offers no evidence for this charge. I've not worked outside anything I know of explicitly mentioned in the *Manual.* I have opposed nothing in the *Manual* references cited in the charge above.

The *Manual* does not condemn my endeavors for loving change.

The work I and others do to love queer people will eventually lead us to propose changes to the *Manual's* Covenant of Christian Conduct. These proposed changes will come through the processes cited in the *Manual.* At present, however, most in the Church of the Nazarene have not been exposed to the arguments and evidence they need to reconsider the statement on human sexuality. Most Nazarenes are ill-informed, so preparatory work needs to be done.

There is nothing in the *Manual* that sets time-frames or time-limits on preparing the members of denomination for change. We're in process, and we're making progress, but change takes time. As a member and minister in the Church of the Nazarene, I am acting in good faith, according to the flexibility provided by the *Manual,* to initiate change.

I did not work outside agreed-upon procedures and processes in the *Manual.*

4. "Resisted the surrender of his credentials." Specifically, Rev. Oord resisted the surrender his credentials when asked by the District Superintendent. Rev. Oord answered the below question and signed documents at his ordination in 1992. *"If after you have been ordained by the Church of the Nazarene you find you cannot conform to the standards, doctrines, and government of said church*

*or wholeheartedly support the church in its missions, will
you voluntarily surrender your credentials and withdraw
from the ministry without charges or trail?"* Rev. Oord
would have been required to answer "YES" to be ordained to the following question (Ordination applica-
tion 1991).

My response: This charge is false.

At no time did Shaw say, "I want your credentials." At
no time did I say, "I will not surrender my credentials." I
have never resisted the surrender of my credentials.

When I saw this charge, I sent a note to Shaw asking for
clarification. In his response, he confirmed my suspicion
that this charge refers to conversations in which he pre-
sented me with accusations/charges and asked if I would
seek a hearing/trial. I chose to defend myself. Choosing
to defend myself is not "resisting the surrender of his credentials." The Manual specifically states that every minister has the right to a fair and impartial hearing, and that
every minister is entitled to the presumption of innocence
(Manual 616).

This charge should alert those hearing my case just
how weak the evidence is against me. When deciding to
defend myself is considered "resisting the surrender of credentials," we see the foolishness of these charges.

Something is amiss when standing for love is considered conduct unbecoming a minister.

If this charge is saying that I agreed when ordained
thirty years ago to surrender my credentials if I could not

conform to the church's standards, doctrines, and government, I respond that those aspects in the *Manual* have changed significantly since my ordination. Ministers who agree to "conform" and "support" are not saying they will forevermore affirm *the exact Manual statements* in circulation when they are ordained.

No general superintendent, district superintendent, or ordained elder I know surrenders credentials each time a general assembly alters the *Manual*. In fact, some of us have played key roles in changing the *Manual*. And it will undoubtedly be altered in the future. Those who work for change, whether successful or not, are not asked to surrender their credentials.

To "conform" and "support" the church is compatible with seeking loving change.

5. "Willfully and actively taught and promoted agenda contrary to the doctrines…" Specifically, through multiple channels of social media platforms, Rev. Oord has willfully and actively taught and promoted an agenda which are contrary to the doctrines of the Church of the Nazarene (*Manual* 600, 606). "Taught and promoted ideas, beliefs, and doctrine out of harmony with… Human Sexuality… in Covenant of Christian Conduct." Specifically, on various dates through multiple social media channels, Rev. Oord has taught and promoted ideas, beliefs, and doctrine out of harmony with the essential statements of the Church of the Nazarene regarding Human Sexuality, as stated in the Covenant of Christian Conduct, paragraph 31.

My response: These charges are false and misleading.

In a later section of my response, I'll address the false claim that I am teaching and promoting an agenda contrary to church "doctrines." The *Manual* does not consider the statement on human sexuality a doctrine, and neither has theologians throughout history. The key issue in these charges seems to be my use of "multiple social media channels."

I find nothing in the *Manual* that forbids using media platforms to foster change. *Manual* paragraphs noted in this charge do not prohibit various channels and social media platforms. Besides, in the contemporary world, savvy lovers use social media to advance the cause of love. The claim that my conduct is unbecoming does not have *Manual* support.

I find this charge especially frustrating. On many occasions, I have asked District Superintendent Shaw to host district-wide or denomination-wide conferences to help Nazarenes think through queer issues. I and others call for *real* dialogue, not people periodically trotted out by leadership to support the denomination's current views. I argued for in-person education on queer issues. Shaw ignored my requests.

Because Shaw and other denominational leaders fail to host discussions of this important issue, Alexa Oord and I hosted an online conference on the Church of the Nazarene and LGBTQ+ concerns. The conference featured contributors to *Why the Church of the Nazarene Should be Fully LGBTQ+ Affirming*. To complain about an internet conference and social media but refuse to host in-person events suggests that Shaw and other leaders are afraid conversations will go directions they don't personally endorse or can't control. It suggests a lack of courage.

I should not be punished for hosting key discussions that few have the courage to host.

6. "Failed to embrace the organizational structure and polity…" and failed "to show due regard for the united advice of the DS and DAB." Specifically, on multiple dates and meetings, Rev. Oord has failed to embrace the organizational structure and polity of the Church of the Nazarene by failing to comply with Section 538.2 of the *Manual*, which states: "A member of the clergy shall always show due regard for the united advice of the District Superintendent and the District Advisory Board." Rev. Oord's failure to be accountable to leadership and the organizational structure of the Church of the Nazarene has caused division and disunity.

My response: I have shown due regard for the advice of the DS and DAB.

In a New Testament story, Jesus' followers are criticized for eating on the Sabbath. Defending them, Jesus says, "The Sabbath was made for humans, not humans for the Sabbath" (Mk. 2:27). His point: rules should serve the human good. When rules don't help, we should break them, because doing good is more important than following rules.

District Superintendent Shaw gave me little advice on how I might encourage the denomination to change its statement on human sexuality. What he did say was vague. Neither Pastor Sarah Riley nor the Real Life Community Church of the Nazarene board members, with whom Shaw spoke, understood what Shaw wanted from me. (See church board letters among appendices.) When I asked Shaw if he required me to be silent on queer concerns, he said he was not silencing me. He cautioned me to be wise, a caution with no specific examples or boundaries.

Shaw made it clear, however, he did not think the statement on human sexuality needed changing. He failed to comprehend why the *Manual* harms queer people. He is an opponent rather than an ally to the work of love I do. It's no surprise that Shaw did not support me, gave little advice, and was vague.

I gave due regard to District Superintendent Shaw's advice. I gave due regard to the advice of the District Advisory Board, which Shaw filtered to me. (I have never met with the board.) I carefully considered all I heard. In giving due regard, I embraced the organizational structure and polity of the denomination stated in the *Manual*. I am not guilty of doing otherwise.

Because Shaw fails to see why a change to the statement on human sexuality is needed, I sometimes did not follow his (vague) advice. I gave it due regard but found it inadequate. Because Shaw is an opponent to the love I think must be expressed, he was not helpful.

Every Nazarene ought to give allegiance first to God and allegiance second to human leaders or organizations.

After all, sometimes leaders and organizations fail to discern well the will of God. Sometimes the advice of authorities undermines the common good. According to Jesus, everyone ought to ignore rules that draw us away from love rather than toward it.

When a leader's advice undermines love, no one should follow it.

I consider my actions to align with the Church of the Nazarene's history of advocating for those at the margins. The very name "Nazarene" identifies Jesus as one who was marginalized and who loved marginalized others. Today, queer people are some of the most ostracized and vulnerable. I try to love like Jesus, and I want love to shape the denomination's structures, polity, beliefs, and practices. When loving LGBTQ+ people is considered "failing to embrace organizational structure and polity," the structure and polity ought to be questioned.

Those serving as my judges must also consider Jesus' teaching. According to him, the good of the people comes before structures or polity. Doing good is more important than following district superintendents or the *Manual*. The *Manual* should support rather than oppose the love to which God calls us all. Specifically…

The *Manual* was meant for humans, not humans for the *Manual*.

7. "Published his responses to Investigative Committee questions…in opposition to Covenant of Christian Conduct…" and "continues to activity promote [contrary] teaching." Specifically, in February 2022, Rev.

Oord published his responses to the Investigative Committee's questions based to his opinions, teaching, and promotion of his viewpoints on Human Sexuality in opposition to the Church of the Nazarene regarding Human Sexuality, as stated in the Covenant of Christian Conduct, paragraph 31. Rev. Oord continues to actively promote this teaching. "Published a book titled *Why the Church of the Nazarene Should be Fully LGBTQ+ Affirming.*" Specifically, on April 14, 2023, Rev. Oord has published a book titled *Why the Church of the Nazarene should be fully LGBTQ+ Affirming.*

My response: The *Manual* does not forbid publishing material aimed at educating Nazarenes.

I'm addressing two charges here, because they're nearly identical. As stated, both identify the document I wrote for the investigative committee in response to accusations. My document was published in a book I co-edited with Alexa Oord called *Why the Church of the Nazarene Should be Fully LGBTQ+ Affirming.* (See the appendices for this document.)

I find nothing in the *Manual* that forbids publishing material that helps the denomination become more loving. Unfortunately, many Nazarenes are unaware of the damage done by denomination's stance on human sexuality. Queer people are harmed. To be alerted to this harm and how they can change, Nazarenes need to be educated. Because LGBTQ+ issues are emotionally charged and the threat of discipline is real, few scholars or leaders dare to educate Nazarenes on queer matters.

Why the Church of the Nazarene Should be Fully LGBTQ+ Affirming moves the denomination toward inclusive love. Queer people wrote some of the 90+ essays, and many tell stories of how the church has hurt them. Allies wrote other essays, explaining why we need to love LGBTQ+ people. Experts in the Bible, theology, law, and more wrote essays. Many explain why arguments supporting the current *Manual* statement on human sexuality are unsatisfying. Others explain why the full affirmation of queer people is biblically and theologically justified.

The "evidence" against me also says, "since his written response to the DAB was initially prepared in February of 2022, Rev. Oord has been active in distributing that document to third parties. In doing so, Rev. Oord has again misrepresented the action of the Intermountain District Advisory Board."

I did share my document. But I fail to see how distributing my defense—which I wrote—amounts to misrepresenting the District Advisory Board's action. My document promotes my ideas, not the DAB's, and it educates Nazarenes on this crucial set of issues.

Rather than charge me with conduct unbecoming a minister for publishing the book and defense document, the Church of the Nazarene ought to thank me and other writers for fostering this crucial conversation. The numerous positive responses to these writings from queer people and allies are evidence the conversation is needed. Many pastors express thanks for the book, and most young Nazarenes I meet are thrilled by it. I predict when the Church of the Nazarene eventually becomes a fully affirming denomination, this book and its contributors will be cited as key instigators of positive transformation.

It would be tragic to convict me for assisting the loving changes already on the way.

I am Not Teaching Against Doctrine

The second charge claims I engaged in "teaching doctrines out of harmony with the doctrinal statements of the Church of the Nazarene." I *have* worked to encourage change to the denomination's statement on human sexuality found in the Covenant of Christian Conduct. But this Covenant has not been and should not be considered "doctrine." So...

My response: This charge is false.

In the Spring of 2023, a document signed by the Board of General Superintendents claimed that the Covenant of Christian Conduct should be considered as essential as the Articles of Faith. This ill-advised directive tried to erase the denomination's longstanding belief that members have liberty in non-essential matters. The Church of the Nazarene has *never* considered its ethical statements in the *Manual* to be essential. I suspect legal consultants initiated this misguided directive, because I know of no trained theologian who would recommend the Covenant of Christian Conduct be considered doctrine.

Fortunately, delegates to the 2023 General Assembly rejected the foolish attempt to raise the Covenant of Christian Conduct to the status of doctrine. The assembly's Resolution JUD-811A attempted to insert the Covenant into the *Manual's* disciplinary portion related to teaching doctrines out of harmony with the church. (See General Assembly document among the appendices). It was defeated in committee and on the assembly floor. The resolution's failure effectively negates the Spring 2023 statement.

The Covenant of Christian Conduct is not doctrine.

There are many reasons *not* to consider the statement on human sexuality "doctrine." Some come from the *Manual* itself. For instance, the *Manual* distinguishes between doctrines in the Articles of Faith and statements like the one on human sexuality. In its language, the *Manual* separates "doctrine" from "practices," "polity," and the Covenant of Christian Conduct:

- **231.3:** "…full acceptance of the doctrines, the Covenant of Christian Character and the Covenant of Christian Conduct, and the polity of the Church:…"

- **28.1:** "…the doctrines and covenants of the church may be known and…"

- **113.11:** "…the doctrines, polity, and practices of the Church of the Nazarene…"

- **145; 146:** "…the doctrines, polity, and practices of the Church of the Nazarene…"

> **Forward:** "…including doctrinal tenets of faith and time-tested standards of morality…"

This sample fits the longstanding practice of distinguishing doctrines from other concerns in the *Manual*. On this issue, Nazarenes often cite a line attributed to Phineas Bresee: "In essentials, unity; in nonessentials, liberty; in all things, charity."

The failure of the General Assembly resolution to make the conduct portion part of doctrine rightly returns the denomination to limiting "doctrine" to the Articles of Faith. Neither the *Manual* nor the history of its interpretation considers statements like the one on human sexuality "essential." So it is false to say I have been teaching against church doctrine.

I have not been teaching against doctrinal statements of the Church of the Nazarene.

Acquit or Convict?

The above arguments should convince those who care about love to acquit me. They should convince those who care about due process to find me not guilty. And because the alleged evidence fails to meet the burden of proof beyond a reasonable doubt, I should be acquitted.

Whether acquitted or convicted, however, I will live a life of love. And even if I'm not credentialed, my love will affect the denomination's members, institutions, and policies. The Church of the Nazarene cannot ignore the love that I and others have for queer people.

Litigation cannot stop love.

A verdict that removes my credentials sends harmful messages. To queer people, it sends the message they are not welcome in the Church of the Nazarene. The *Manual* statement on human sexuality already says this, of course, but a guilty verdict will accentuate it. Do you want to tell roughly 5-7% of the world's population they are not welcome?

To the allies of queer people, a guilty message says, "your love for queer people is prohibited." It says, "we know what's good for your queer loved ones; you don't." Do you want to tell supportive friends, family, and other allies—a group that likely includes over 50% of the population—the Church of the Nazarene does not endorse their love?

A guilty verdict sends a message to young people—both queer and allies—that the denomination has no room for them. If recent polling is correct, most young Nazarenes think about queer matters like I do. They're affirming. (See statistics in my defense document.) For decades, the Church of the Nazarene has suffered a silent schism as young people leave. The holiness movement is among the worst of any religion at retaining their youth. Do you want more future leaders of the denomination, especially young people in North America and Europe, to renounce the Nazarene family?

A guilty verdict sends a message to ordained elders who love queer people that their ministry and livelihood are in jeopardy. That's the message many received from the verdict of Dee Kelly's trial. Guilty verdicts promote a litigation culture; they embolden gate-keepers like the Holiness Partnership. Do you want to usher in an inquisition era?

Do you want to be known for suppressing healthy conversations on the most important issues of our time? Would you like to be remembered as someone who prosecuted ministers and theologians for seeking to love the most vulnerable? Do you want exclusion to be your legacy?

I Aim to Love

I urge you to exonerate me. I admonish you to encourage healthy dialogue about how we all might embody Jesus's *agape* love. And join me and others who seek change to the Church of the Nazarene's statement on human sexuality.

The *Manual* prescribes a high bar for judging an accused person guilty. Paragraph 616 puts it this way: "Every accused is entitled to the presumption of innocence until proven guilty. As to each charge and specification, the prosecution shall have the burden of *proving guilt to a moral certainty* and *beyond a reasonable doubt*." (Italics added.) I cannot see how *anyone* hearing my case can honestly say I am guilty of conduct unbecoming a minister and teaching doctrines contrary to the *Manual* to "a moral certainty and beyond a reasonable doubt."

I and many others believe the Holy Spirit is calling the Church of the Nazarene to change its views on queer matters. As an extension of the love that Jesus compels us to express for the widow, foreigner, and outsider, I and others also love queer people. We believe the Spirit is calling the denomination to the love at the heart its holiness message.

The words of Gamaliel are appropriate for those who judge me and others who think like me. When speaking at a trial of Christians seeking change, Gamaliel says, "In the present case I advise you: Leave these people alone! Let them go! For if their purpose or activity is of human origin, it will fail. But if it is from God, you will not be able to stop them; you will find yourselves fighting against God" (Acts 5:38-39).

Those who hear my case and similar ones should "leave alone" and "let go" me and others brought up on charges for loving queer people. But whatever you decide…

I aim to love.

ACKNOWLEDGEMENTS:

I am in debt to many for their advice and suggestions when I was writing this document. This statement is much better because of their help. I would like to acknowledge each by name, but doing so may put each in jeopardy. I look forward to the day acknowledgements of gratitude and conversations can occur without worry of punishment. Sadly, this trial is evidence that day has not yet come.

I'm also indebted to the 90+ courageous essayists in *Why the Church of the Nazarene Should be Fully LGBTQ+ Affirming*. Their writings offer powerful insights and cogent arguments. They and the book are hopeful signs that the denomination can lovingly embrace queer people. For their essays, get a copy of the book or visit lovingnazarenes.com.

Appendices:

THOMAS JAY OORD'S RESPONSE
to Accusations Brought by Signatories Outside the Intermountain District but Reformulated by an Intermountain District Board

What follows are my responses to questions listed at the conclusion of this document. The questions were formulated by a committee from the Church of the Nazarene's Intermountain District after considering six broad accusations against me made by a group of 10 or so signatories. The people in this accusing group are not members of the Intermountain District but sent their accusations to District Superintendent Scott Shaw. After he talked with General Superintendent Fili Chambo, Shaw moved forward with the proceedings.

Superintendent Shaw met with me in November 2021 to relay the original charges. He explained the process and asked what I wanted to do. I said I would face the accusations and undergo the hearing/trial as laid out in the Manual. Superintendent Shaw said he'd choose the committee to hear my case, evaluate my written response, and receive my verbal defense on a date to be determined. He thereafter assembled a district committee and appointed

Assistant District Superintendent Brent Deakins as the chair.

To my mind, the charges against me divide into two parts. One part is theological. The other is about social ethics, specifically the denomination's stance on Lesbian, Gay, Bisexual, Transgender, and Queer (LGBTQ) people outlined in Covenant of Christian Conduct in "Human Sexuality and Marriage."

The committee assigned to my case wisely set aside most theological charges leveled by the accusing group. Those charges revealed a lack of understanding of how the Wesleyan-holiness tradition thinks about salvation, God's love, other religious traditions, and more. The accusing signatories fail to understand the range of acceptable beliefs in the Wesleyan-holiness tradition and the Church of the Nazarene.

Because I consider the theological charges without basis, I'll address them first and rather briefly. I'll deal with questions about LGBTQ people and the denomination's view of Human Sexuality and Marriage later. I regard the latter issues as the primary reasons I am undergoing this hearing/trial. Those issues provide an opportunity to explain the meaning and primacy of love in the Wesleyan-holiness theology that undergirds the Church of the Nazarene.

Theological Concerns

• The Church of the Nazarene's Articles of Faith

I appreciate, embrace, affirm, and endorse the Articles of Faith in the Church of the Nazarene.

Occasionally, I am asked why I chose to be ordained in the Church of the Nazarene and choose to remain thirty years after my ordination ceremony. I respond that I'm compelled by the Wesleyan theology undergirding the denomination's articles of faith. No set of statements can perfectly express all one wants to say about God, of course, and the articles are constantly being revised. I appreciate, embrace, affirm, and endorse the Articles of Faith in the Church of the Nazarene. I have no issues with them and see my views as aligned with the articles.

Part of question three below asks, "How do you deal with any discrepancies between your teaching (in public comments, blog posts, conference speaking engagements, etc.) and your harmonious support of the COTN Articles of Faith?" In my view, there are no discrepancies, so I regard the question as misinformed.

My accusers apparently interpret the articles differently than I do. My beliefs and teachings do not align with their views. But I do not see my teaching as leading to discrepancies about valid interpretations of the articles. And many scholars in the Church of the Nazarene interpret the articles in the way I do, especially those with extensive theological education.

I believe my accusers do not sufficiently understand what it means to embrace the Wesleyan-holiness theology that undergirds the Articles of Faith in the Church of the Nazarene. For example, I make statements about truth in other religious traditions that trouble my accusers. Our Wesleyan theology of prevenient grace, however, supports God's work in religions other than Christianity.

The beauty of the Wesleyan tradition is it's understanding that God's love and truth aren't reserved for just a few; they are available to all. I consider the claims of Christianity, however, more true and more winsome than those of other religious traditions.[1] That's the major reason I choose to be a Christian.

Or take my view of the afterlife. My accusers apparently do not understand my stance on this subject and have consequently misrepresented me. They seem not to realize the possibility that no one will be "finally impenitent," to use the statement in the Manual. Wesleyan-holiness people believe God wants to save all. I reject the idea that God *forces everyone* into heaven. I'm not what many call a "classic universalist," because of my view of creaturely freedom, another Wesleyan emphasis. Scripture and the Manual leave open the possibility that God's love will ultimately redeem all creatures through loving persuasion. The Church of the Nazarene is optimistic about the power of God's grace.[2]

• Believing God Exists

I believe God exists. I'm exceedingly surprised by this question.

I'm not certain God exists, however. I doubt anyone can be 100% certain, although I admit some people claim

---

1. For details on my view of God's loving revelation to all creatures, see Thomas Jay Oord, *The Uncontrolling Love of God* (Downers Grove, Ill: Intervarsity Academic, 2015).

2. For details on my view of the afterlife, see Thomas Jay Oord, *Questions and Answers for God Can't* (SacraSage, 2020).

to be. Even if certainty about God's existence is possible, the Manual doesn't require anyone to attain this state of confidence.

Throughout history, Christians have typically steered clear of claiming to be certain about God. We talk instead about having *faith*. Christians are believers, not "certainers," to coin a word.

I don't advocate blind faith, however, and I often argue against it. There are good reasons to believe God exists. The phrases I use to describe my stance are that I "reasonably trust" God exists or think God's existence is "more plausible than not." Those phrases, in my way of thinking, point to good arguments, evidence, and experiences that indicate God exists… requiring no one to be certain.

Incidentally, most people I talk to about this issue find immense encouragement after hearing they can have genuine doubts about God and yet be faithfully Christian. My statement, "I'm not certain," offers them hope. They're relieved to discover Phineas Bresee's words that "Faith isn't the absence of doubt; it's choosing to believe, despite doubt."[3]

• Jesus and God

Christians have throughout the centuries tried to discern how to make sense of Jesus' relation to God. Some

---

3. I explain myself on these matters in a book I co-edited called *Postmodern and Wesleyan?* published by the Nazarene Publishing House. Instead of cutting and pasting paragraphs here, see my essay, "Truth and Postmodernism," among others.

scripture passages say Jesus has a unique relationship with the One he calls "Abba." Biblical writers, over and again, say Jesus reveals God, and I strongly affirm this. In this sense, I believe Jesus is divine. I stand with Scripture and the Manual.

We Christians have various theories for why Jesus did not have the attributes we think characterize God. One that I've cited in many writings says those attributes were set aside in the incarnation. Often, Philippians 2 is the basis for this theory, and I've written extensively about this. It fits what I and other scholars call a "Spirit Christology:" Jesus responded perfectly to the Spirit and revealed God's nature of love.[4] A Trinitarian model that says God is revealed in Jesus makes the most sense to me.

Nearly all Christians think God is omnipresent and omniscient, by which we mean God is present to all creation and God knows all that's possible to know. But Jesus clearly was not omnipresent. And he lacked complete knowledge, illustrated by the questions he often asked and statements made (e.g., "Who touched me?" "No one knows the day and hour, except the Father"). Simply saying "Jesus is God" can be easily interpreted as meaning Jesus was also omnipresent or omniscient, which, according to the Bible, he was not.

I don't recall the specifics of the conversation with Michael McElyea noted in question 4c below. I suspect

---

4. For more on this, see my essay, "Essential Kenosis Christology," in *Christology: From the Wesleys to the Twenty-first Century,* Jason Vicker and Jerome Van Kuiken, eds. (Nashville: Wesley's Foundry Books, 2020) and my book, *The Uncontrolling Love of God* (Downers Grove, Ill.: IVP Academic, 2015).

my point in the exchange was simply to say that while Jesus reveals God, he did not have *all* the attributes many Christians claim God has. But more importantly, I see no conflict between my views and the Manual's statements on Jesus.

I affirm the Article of Faith on Jesus.

Sexuality Concerns

I have for decades worked for changes in the Church of the Nazarene's statements on LGBTQ people, their identities, and sexual practices. In my view, the denominational statements do not reflect well the love at the heart of Wesleyan-holiness theology. I was happy about the progress made in the recent General Assembly rewriting of the "Marriage and Sexuality" statement. But I believe more changes are needed.

My desire to see changes in the Manual comes from my love for God, for members of the Church of the Nazarene, for LGBTQ people, and for the friends and family of LGBTQ people. I think God is pleased by healthy LGBTQ sexual practices and God affirms nonheteronormative identities. I think the Church of the Nazarene ought to imitate God's love by being pleased in the same way.

I am one among a sizable number of members of the Church of the Nazarene who are LGBTQ affirming. I say a "sizable number" because I don't know the exact total. Most affirming members are reluctant to say so in public, although many divulge their beliefs to me in private. By "LGBTQ affirming," I mean many members of the

Church of the Nazarene believe non-heterosexual (e.g., Lesbian, Gay, Bisexual, Transgender, and Queer) orientation, identity, and sexual behavior (expressed in a covenant relationship) are compatible with authentic Christian faith.

As evidence for this claim, I rely upon the Pew Research Center. A 2007 Pew poll showed that 31% of those who identify with the Church of the Nazarene thought society should accept homosexuality. That percentage jumped to 40% by 2014.[5] I suspect the percentage is higher today, but Pew has not released current numbers.

Assuming the USA Church of the Nazarene has around 600,000 members, the Pew polls suggest that 200,000+ US Nazarenes hold views about LGBTQ matters similar to mine. From my conversations with pastors and laity on the Intermountain District, I believe the percentage of affirming people on the district is higher. Even if these polls and estimates are off several percentage points, it remains the case that a sizable number of members of the denomination think society should accept LGBTQ people and their behaviors. Every person I know who thinks society should accept LGBTQ also thinks the denomination should accept it. They have the same standard for love in the church and society.

A Barna Report indicates that 46% of practicing Christians under the age of 40 want more laws to protect

---

5. See https://www.pewresearch.org/fact-tank/2015/12/18/most-u-s-christian-groups-grow-more-accepting-of-homosexuality/

Same-Sex Marriage and LGBTQ rights.[6] This is not the same as saying LGBTQ is compatible with Christian faith, of course, but most who want protections and rights are also LGBTQ affirming. In other words, they think about these matters much like I do. The two major takeaways from that Barna report are 1) American Christians are becoming increasingly accepting of LGBTQ people and their sexual behavior, and 2) younger American Christians are more accepting than older Americans.

Based on the Pew and Barna polls and my own interactions, I suspect most US Nazarene youth want the Church of the Nazarene's views on LGBQT issues to change. And from my time speaking in Europe, I believe the percentage of European Nazarene youth who want change is even higher. If the views of the young eventually become the views of the majority, the Church of the Nazarene will undergo change in the coming decades. We have revised many topics in the Covenant of Christian Conduct over the past century; we should expect and welcome changes related to LGBTQ issues.

My experience speaking at nearly every Church of the Nazarene higher educational institution in the US and many Nazarene institutions overseas tells me that most university students and faculty are LGBTQ affirming. Many talk to me about these matters in private, fearing accusations and the treatment I'm currently undergoing. They want a safe forum without fear of reprisal to make

6. See https://www.barna.com/research/americas-change-of-mind-on-same-sex-marriage-and-lgbtq-rights/

their case for full LGBTQ inclusion in the Church of the Nazarene.[7]

Should I Stay Or Should I Go?

Many people—especially young people and including some pastors—leave the Church of the Nazarene because of its current stance on LGBTQ people. A 2008 poll of twenty religions/denominations said the holiness tradition—of which the Church of the Nazarene is the largest denomination—is the *worst* of all religious groups at retaining young people. Only 32% of Nazarene youth remain with the denomination.[8] A similar poll in 2015 showed no change in this rate of exit.[9]

Some members who want changes on LGBTQ issues ask my advice on whether they should stay or leave. I counsel them on a case-by-case basis. Some leave to become Methodists, Lutherans, Episcopalians, or something else. I respect their decisions, and I wish them well.

Some stay. Despite thinking the denomination's view of human sexuality is unloving, unbiblical, or just out of touch, some LGBTQ-affirming youth, pastors, scholars,

---

7. The call for safe and irenic discussion of LGBTQ issues is also present among Church of the Nazarene clergy. See the doctoral work of Reg Watson on this matter (R. G. Watson, *Nazarene Clergy Responses to Homosexuality and Interactions with LGBT People* [Doctoral dissertation, Regent University, 2015], 123, 125, 279, 317).

8. See http://thomasjayoord.com/index.php/blog/archives/atheists_only_slightly_worse_at_retaining_children_than_holiness_folk

9. See https://www.pewforum.org/2015/05/12/chapter-2-religious-switching-and-intermarriage/pr_15-05-12_rls_chapter2-04/

and leaders remain with the Church of the Nazarene. I respect those decisions too.

Why do some stay, despite disagreeing with the Manual on LGBTQ matters? Here are the reasons I often hear...

1. Family and Friendship

Many LGBTQ-affirming members of the denomination have strong friendship and family ties to people in the Church of the Nazarene. Rather than think beliefs and rules are primary for membership, they think of the denomination as a family or intimate community. As you know, this way of thinking about the church has strong biblical support.

This approach assumes people are more important than rules. Besides, do you leave a family just because other members hold beliefs that you don't... especially when *so many* of your siblings believe as you do? Friendship and family are more important than rules and regulations.

2. Changing Groups

Some who remain are students of denominational history. The Church of the Nazarene has changed its views on many issues, especially issues in the Code of Christian Conduct. Divorce is now considered appropriate in some cases, for instance, although it's still mentioned in the Code alongside same-sex marriage. Jewelry is commonplace today, but was once condemned. Few members today think twice about going to the theater or circus, but these practices were forbidden in the 1928 Manual. The denomination has changed its mind on dancing, movies, and many other topics in the Covenant of Christian Conduct.

Denominational leaders also realize context matters. In some African contexts, we tolerate polygamy among Church of the Nazarene members. In some European contexts, members consume alcohol with no fear of repercussion. Divorce no longer carries the stigma among US Nazarenes it once did.

Groups change, including denominational groups. Why think the Church of the Nazarene will keep its current stance on LGBTQ? We made positive strides at the recent General Assembly to alter the denomination's official view. But we need more changes for the Church of the Nazarene to become fully LGBTQ affirming. Many stay expecting that eventually change will come, hopefully sooner rather than later. The optimism of grace leads me to believe the denomination will eventually see that love calls it to embrace and affirm LGBTQ people.

3. Loving Experience

Others believe the denomination's theology implies that LGBTQ people and their loving practices ought to be affirmed. Like me, some cite love as the core of the holiness message. Others consider religious experience vital for discerning authentic Christian faith. They know LGBTQ people who have vibrant Christian testimonies.

Those who oppose LGBTQ people and activity often reference seven or eight biblical verses to support their view. Biblical scholars, theologians, and Christian ethicists have written massive tomes on this material. Many argue those verses either apply to ancient practices not identical to contemporary LGBTQ issues or those verses reflect cultural biases of their day. The biblical witness to sex and marriage is complex.[10]

---

10. Among the helpful books and essays on this subject, see Cheryl B. *Anderson, Ancient Laws and Contemporary Controversies: The Need for Inclusive Biblical Interpretation* (Oxford University Press 2009); John Boswell, *Christianity, Social Tolerance, and Homosexuality* (University of Chicago Press, 1980); James V. Brownson, *Bible, Gender, Sexuality: Reframing the Church's Debate on Same-Sex Relationships* (William B. Eerdmans, 2013); Elizabeth M. Edman, *Queer Virtue: What LGBTQ People Know about Life and Love and How it Can Revitalize Christianity* (Beacon, 2016); Richard Elliott Friedman and Shawna Dolansky, eds. *The Bible Now: Homosexuality, Abortion, Women, Death Penalty, Earth* (Oxford: Oxford University Press, 2011); Victor Paul Furnish, "Homosexuality?" in *The Moral Teaching of Paul: Selected Issues*, 3rd ed. (Nashville: Abingdon, 2009), 55-93; David Gushee, *Changing Our Minds*, 2nd ed. (Spirit Books, 2015); Karen R. Keen, *Scripture, Ethics, and the Possibility of Same-Sex Relationships* (William B. Eerdmans, 2018); Craig S. Keener, *Romans: A New Covenant Commentary* (Cascade, 2009); Colby Martin, *Unclobber: Rethinking Our Misuse of the Bible On Homosexuality* (Westminster John Knox, 2016); Dale B. Martin, *Sex and the Single Savior* (Westminster John Knox, 2006); Russell Pregeant, *Engaging the New Testament* (Minneapolis: Fortress, 1995); Eugene F. Rogers, "Same-sex Complementarity: A Theology of Marriage" (The Christian Century, 2011); Robin Scroggs, *The New Testament and Homosexuality* (Philadelphia: Fortress, 1983); Matthew Vines, *God and The Gay Christian: The Biblical Case in Support of Same-Sex Relationships* (Convergent, 2014).

Many people in the Church of the Nazarene already endorse this general approach to biblical interpretation when defending the full status of women in ministry. In fact, we could cite more biblical passages that relegate women to subservient roles than verses condemning LGBTQ people and behavior. And yet the Church of the Nazarene rightly privileges Scriptures that support full status for women in ministry and equality in marriage.[11] Many of the passages cited call for love and equality for *all* people. Love and lived experience matter, and we should use this hermeneutic for LGBTQ concerns.

The Theological Difference

Other members of the Church of the Nazarene ask me if they should leave because of theological differences with the denomination. Those differences are not with the Human Sexuality and Marriage statements; they disagree with the Articles of Faith. I tell them the articles were not handed down from heaven, and each allows for a range of interpretation. The articles have also changed over time, at least to some degree. Articles 15 and 16 are currently going through a major overhaul, and the future will bring more changes.

---

11. On the role culture plays in discerning LGBTQ matters, see Rev. Bruce Barnard, "Cognitive Dissonance and the Progression of the Church on Major Cultural Norms," (D.Min., George Fox University, 2016).

Many say their theological views differ drastically from the articles. Some believe, for instance, the denomination's view on biblical inerrancy is too soft. They want a Manual statement that affirms absolute biblical inerrancy. Others think the Articles are at odds with the sovereignty of God. They believe God is in control and we have no freedom to do other than what God decides. Some think the Articles of Faith are wrong about hell, original sin, women in ministry, sanctification as transformation, or something else.

In these conversations, I realize some members of the denomination actually want a Calvinist or Catholic theology. Or something else. So I lovingly tell them to consider joining another community.

Am I wrong to encourage some to leave but encourage some LGBTQ-affirming members to stay?

I don't think so. As I see it, the essential theology of the Church of the Nazarene is compatible with believing LGBTQ people are welcome in the denomination. Here's what I mean:

The core of our holiness message is love. "Love" doesn't mean, "we accept any behavior or beliefs whatsoever." It means we want the well-being of others. We seek the transformation of ourselves and all creation. Some LGBTQ behavior—including same-sex marriage—can promote well-being. It's good and healthy; it represents the values of the Kingdom of God. The transformation God desires rarely if ever requires LGBTQ people to change their sexual orientation, identity, or loving behavior.

Let me put this another way: LGBTQ people can live Christlike lives. Some of the most loving people I know are not heteronormative. Living Christlike lives is the holiness gospel, and some LGBTQ people act like Christ. They love like Jesus loved. And their identity or behavior as LGBTQ people is not an obstacle to their being Christlike.

Love calls us to be faithful in our partnering commitments. Those who commit to monogamy—whether heterosexual or same-sex marriage—are called to be faithful to God, their partner, and the Kingdom. If the Church of the Nazarene—as people who seek purity—wants to encourage loving faithfulness and discourage promiscuity, it ought to endorse same-sex marriage. The denomination also ought to lead the way in advocating for transgender people. It ought to recognize the variation of attraction experienced by bisexual people. And so on.

As those who care for the marginalized, Nazarenes ought to be allies for LGBTQ people rather than adversaries.

My Role as a Licensed Minister and Thought Leader

Some questions at the conclusion of this document come from the district committee and not from the original charges against me. These questions pertain to how I see my role as an acting minister and thought leader in the Church of the Nazarene.

One set of questions asks about officiating same-sex marriages. Given what I've said above, it will come as no surprise that I look forward to the day the denomination endorses same-sex marriage. If members of the Church of the Nazarene truly believe in sexual purity, they ought to encourage lifelong sexual partnerships in marriage. The holiness message ought to compel members of the denomination to support same-sex marriage.

I have never officiated a same-sex marriage, and I have no plans to do so. But if one of my daughters was a lesbian and wanted me to officiate her marriage to her lesbian partner, I'd do it in a heartbeat. If needed, I'd officiate the ceremony as a layperson and ask the couple to get an official marriage endorsement from a state official. But I love my children and think this love far exceeds any commitment I have to a statement in the Covenant of Christian Conduct I think needs changing. I hope all clergy would privilege love for their children over denominational rules, even if it comes at personal cost. And if they would, they likely understand much of the LGBTQ logic I'm presenting here.

I do *not* think ordained elders should surrender their credentials if they officiate a same-sex wedding. Our allegiance is first to God and the love to which God calls. But because most members in the Church of the Nazarene currently do not think about same-sex weddings the way I do, I'd encourage the Nazarene elder who wants to officiate a same-sex ceremony to do so and subsequently have it endorsed by some other person or agency. Or do so with a minister of another Christian denomination. I give this advice with a sad heart, however, believing that on this issue, those outside the Church of the Nazarene are more in tune with the Spirit's leading.

The final set of questions asks about my personal beliefs and the denomination's. It asks if I support the denomination and whether I'm in "hearty accord" with the statement on human sexuality. I strongly support the denomination; I love the people who comprise this community. I've given much of my time, emotional energy, and resources to help the Church of the Nazarene broadly and to help individual members specifically. To use the language of the Apostle Paul, I have "poured myself out" sacrificially for this body of believers.

I heartily support and believe myself to be in accord with the Articles of Faith. But I think the denomination's statement of human sexuality should evolve. I will continue working to see changes made. That will mean speaking against current denominational practices and ideas I believe are not aligned with our core theology of love. I expect all people associated with the Church of the Nazarene—whether they are ordained or not—to place their allegiance with the God of love and see allegiance to the Church of the Nazarene as secondary. God and denomination are not identical.

I would also expect people who disagree with the Covenant of Christian Conduct to do so respectfully. And to be discerning in how they disagree. I don't claim to have always been wise, but I feel good about most of my speech and activities. I commit myself to working for change in wise and loving ways. I aim to love in word and deed.

THE PROCESS OF CHANGE IN THE CHURCH OF THE NAZARENE

In 2007, I gave a plenary paper at Northwest Nazarene University's Wesley Center Conference. The paper was titled, "Revisioning Article X: Fifteen Changes in the Church of the Nazarene's Article on Entire Sanctification." In my presentation and the paper that circulated widely thereafter, I suggested both major and minor changes to the denomination's views on sanctification.

No one brought me up on charges. No one thought I was a heretic or was teaching false doctrine when I suggested *fifteen* changes to the article widely regarded as the denomination's distinctive doctrine. In fact, many fellow scholars applauded my suggestions, while suggesting changes of their own or noting differences in nuance. An official denominational committee formed soon thereafter, and years later, several of my suggested changes occurred.

Before this event, I suggested a change to Article I in the Manual, the article on the doctrine of God. I suggested we should add a statement about God's love. My suggestion made its way through the system and now is part of the official statement. Again, no one brought me up on charges for thinking the Articles of Faith needed changing.

To be clear, I'm not claiming I *alone* orchestrated these changes to the Manual. Others played key roles; it takes a community. But I bring up these examples to note that even with the Articles of Faith—which are widely thought *essential* rather than nonessential like the Covenant of Christian Conduct—differences of opinion can lead to changes in denomination's official views. Someone—or many someones—initiates conversations leading to those changes.

It's also important to note that not *all* of my proposed changes were accepted. But no one said, "the new Manual doesn't reflect *everything* Tom suggested, so he should leave." Nor did I feel compelled to abandon the denomination. Apparently, differences of opinion are acceptable for the Articles of Faith. How much more should a difference of opinion be acceptable to the denomination's Covenant of Christian Conduct? While Covenant issues are important, they are *not* essential.

Far better to follow the advice of Phineas Bresee and many others: "On essentials, we seek unity. On nonessentials, we allow freedom. In all things, we seek to love."

How Does Change Come?

According to the polls I've cited and my experience, a huge number of Church of the Nazarene members agree with me. Probably hundreds of thousands. But the majority do not. Some districts or world regions are more "progressive" on this issue. But the majority currently does not think like me and many, many others.

If the change I want to see is to become a reality, how will that occur? What brings people to change their minds about LGBTQ people and issues to endorse views like mine?

Most people who change their minds do not suddenly realize the few biblical passages that directly pertain to same-sex relations don't apply today. Change rarely comes through biblical argumentation, as important as Scripture is.

Change comes when people we know well—our children, best friends, or family members—"come out" as lesbian, gay, bisexual, transgender, queer, or something similar. Close relationships also lead many to realize LGBTQ identity, attractions, and behaviors can be healthy and loving. A growing number of members of the Church of the Nazarene are experiencing these perspective-changing encounters with family and friends.

Others change their minds on issues of human sexuality when they spend time with LGBTQ Christians who love like Jesus. These people may not be family members or friends, but they clearly live lives of love. "The proof of the pudding is in the eating," says the adage, and the proof is that many LGBTQ people live fruitful lives of the Spirit. They are transformed into the image of the invisible God.

When I think of those people in my own life, friends like Alicia, Carol, Cindy, David, Dwayne, Flora, Fraser, Gary, Isaac, John, Jordan, Lisa, Manuel, Matthew, Michael, Monica, Scott, Susie, Tim, Tyler, and more come to mind. LGBTQ people show evidence of the gifts of ministry, pastoral leadership, and general good works in the world.

Still others change their minds on intellectual grounds. That's how I changed my mind. Through a study of scripture, theology, science, and more, some people come to realize traditional binary views of human sexuality do not apply to all people. It's no minor point that the consensus opinion in psychology and other human sciences is that LGBTQ behavior can be healthy and life-giving.[12] Scientific consensus is on the side of people who think like

---

12. I could cite numerous sources to support this claim. But here's a link to the American Psychological Association statements on LGBTQ issues https://www.apa.org/topics/lgbtq/

me about LGBTQ issues. Those who point to examples of LGBTQ misbehavior—e.g., abuse, promiscuity, unsafe sex—often fail to note this misbehavior also occurs among heterosexuals.

What *won't* happen is that every single member of the Church of the Nazarene awakes one morning and simultaneously says, "we should change the statement on human sexuality and marriage today." Instead, change takes time. In the beginning, there are a few dissenters. Momentum builds. And eventually, the majority see the need to alter official statements. It's a process, and if the statistics I offered and my experiences are correct, the Church of the Nazarene is changing its views on LGBTQ issues.

In fact, change is already here. It's just that many members of the Church of the Nazarene are afraid to make the public statements I make. They know negative repercussions will probably come if they speak out or ask for civil conversation. But I predict many will become more vocal in the coming days. The issues at the heart of my case are likely to grow in importance.

WHERE SHOULD WE GO FROM HERE?

I know the decisions this Intermountain District committee makes carry real and widespread consequences. If the committee endorses and wholeheartedly affirms what I say, those who believe traditional views about sexuality and marriage will be angry. Some may leave the denomination.

If the committee rejects what I say and votes to take my license, those who want change will be angry. Pastors and laity will leave the Church of the Nazarene. Others will go into hiding, fearing that speaking out will mean their trial and dismissal. Rejecting the way forward I have proposed—opening up a conversation about accepting people with LGBTQ identity, orientation, and loving sexual behaviors—means more Nazarene youth will leave.

It's not too dramatic to say the denomination's future vitality is at stake.

I trust that those hearing my case will find my theological views within the spectrum of viable interpretations of the Articles of Faith. I certainly think they are, and so do many others.

Ideally, the committee would join me in seeking changes in the statement on Marriage and Human Sexuality. Even if committee members do not take a proactive approach to make changes, I hope they see the Covenant of Christian Conduct as a nonessential document. There is room for those who in good conscience and in the name of love disagree with the denomination's statement on marriage and human sexuality.

I hope the committee will also see the need for open conversations about LGBTQ issues. People want to speak freely and without fear of dismissal from their leadership roles or the denomination. My case could spark healthy discussions.[13]

---

13. I am grateful to wise friends who read previous drafts of this document and give helpful advice. Because some could receive criticism for being associated with me or this document, I'll not list their names. But I'm *deeply* grateful for their kindness, encouragement, and suggestions.

Above all, I hope this committee will stand for what, in my mind, is the way of love.

REV. DR. THOMAS JAY OORD (January 2022)

Questions for Dr. Thomas Jay Oord

1. Do you affirm and support the statement in the Nazarene manual on Human Sexuality and Marriage (31)?

   If not, what areas are of concern for you and why?

   If yes, help us understand how your statements in the evidence (Exhibit 1 & 4) and your personal beliefs about human sexuality are in harmony or are not in harmony with the doctrine of the COTN? Specifically, your comments stating:

   a. "I am one among those who thinks it (homosexual activity) is not always sinful" (Exhibit 1)

   b. When asked the question: "Should Ministers of the COTN should be allowed to marry LGBTQ couples?" You responded: "Yes on the first." Do you believe Nazarene ministers should be allowed to perform same-sex ceremonies? If you were asked to do a same-sex ceremony, would you do it? In your view, would performing a same-sex ceremony be a violation of the COTN beliefs and be cause for surrendering of ordination credentials? How are your publicly stated views and opinions concerning same-sex marriages consistent and in accord with the COTN statements on human sexuality?

2. What do you mean by "full inclusion" with your view and stance on same-sex sexuality? (Exhibit 1: "I am in favor of full inclusion of LGBTQ people…") For which of the following roles are you in favor of a same-sex sexually active person being eligible to serve in the Church of the Nazarene? As an Ordinated minister? As a non-ordained minister? As a member? In an elected Leadership position? As a lay teacher? As an attender? Other? Does your position on "full inclusion" also include marriage ceremonies bless and sanctioned by the COTN?

3. Do you affirm and support Articles 1-16 in the Nazarene manual?

If not, what areas are of concern for you and why?

If yes, how do you deal with any discrepancies between your teaching (in public comments, blog posts, conference speaking engagements, etc.) and your harmonious support of the COTN Articles of Faith?

4. Help us understand your statements on the certainty in the existence of God and your understanding of Articles 1, 2 and 3.

a. Specifically you say in a blog "But I'm not 100% sure God exists…" (footnote 9 on pg. 5 of accusation document). Are you now certain in the existence of God as stated in Article 1, 2 and 3?

b. Exhibit 5 "I know few scholars who think the only people who can rightly self-identify as Christians are those who think Jesus is God." Are you one of those scholars? If so, help us understand how someone can be a Christian without believing that Jesus is God. (Article 2)

c. Do you remember or have documentation on the conversation in Exhibit 5 with Michael McElyea? His comment states that you told Michael that "you told me that you do not even believe that Jesus is God Himself." Does this comment accurately reflect what you said and what you believe personally? Or what did you mean by that implied statement? Do you believe that Jesus is God as stated in Article 2?

5. How do you differentiate your personal beliefs and role as an ordained minister in the COTN and your role as a teacher in the COTN? What responsibility do you have as a Nazarene minister supporting the COTN and respecting the office of an ordained elder for the public/online statements that you make? How do your public/online statements and teachings demonstrate that you are in hearty accord with the statements of the COTN on human sexuality?

LETTERS FROM REAL LIFE
COMMUNITY CHURCH OF
THE NAZARENE

Rev. Scott Shaw
District Superintendent
Intermountain District
Church of the Nazarene

Dear Rev. Shaw,

Following recent events we, the Real Life Community
Church of the Nazarene board, have been notified of Rev.
Tom Oord's change of assignment status with RLCC and
some of the context which led up to this decision. We
value Rev. Oord's participation in our church body and
the care that he shows to our community in helping lead
us to a deeper and richer relationship with God, with each
other, and with creation.

We have the responsibility at present to notify the rest of
the church body of this decision in a way that is whole-
some, forthright and respectful of the individuals and

issues involved, as well as the institution of the Church of the Church of the Nazarene. And as we look to this effort and plan the future of our staff after this probationary period, we would ask for clarification on two specific points.

1. Specifically, which steps taken by Rev. Oord were inappropriate in "promoting information that is in conflict with the Covenant of Christian Conduct?"

2. After the designated period, what would be criteria for appropriate behavior that would allow us to consider restoring Rev. Oord as an associate pastor at RLCC?

We invite you to meet with us as a board to respond to our questions in person as we want to make sure we make space for clarity and understanding.

We are aware that you have a number of pressing responsibilities over the next few weeks, but as this decision has immediate effect, we would prefer not to delay communicating with the church body any longer than necessary. We have established a timeline of June for meeting with the rest of the church, and would appreciate your responses before that time.

Respectfully,

The RLCC Board
Mary Beth Hanson, Michael Whiting, Julianna Poe, Michael Vernor

Rev. Scott Shaw
District Superintendent
Intermountain District
Church of the Nazarene

Dear Rev. Shaw,

Thank you for taking the time to meet with us on Saturday
and answer our questions regarding the incident with Rev.
Oord. After our conversation together we now recognize
that the reasons and motivation for this discipline of Rev.
Oord were relational in nature. We also understand that
this situation is multi-faceted, and that as the District
Superintendent you are tasked with balancing numerous
relationships and responsibilities.

We as a board continued the conversation following our
time with you and Brent, and we both respect the position
you were in, and are simultaneously disappointed with the
disciplinary tone of the action that was taken. While we
realize this letter will not change your decision, we feel the
need to express for the record our preference for reconciliation toward restored relationship and our dissatisfac-
tion with the lack of a clear path to such reconciliation for
Rev. Oord.

During our meeting you mentioned three steps toward
reconciliation. We would like to see the specific steps com-
municated with Rev. Oord and our church board.

As we look at the scripture we find numerous examples of those who questioned the Status Quo, including Jesus. Both then and now we find that the 97% are not always on the right side of history or of the God who loves and justifies all who call on his name. And while we affirm the purpose of denominations clearly establishing sets of beliefs in order to minimize infighting, we also see God promoting relationships over rules.

Ultimately, we both support those who affirm the position of the Church of the Nazarene as set forth in 2017, as well as those who seek to change that position and exemplify God's Love to everyone. We value Rev. Oord's openness as he wrestles with the implications of that Incomprehensible Love lived out in everyday action, and we hope that you will take that intention into account when this matter is revisited in the future.

Respectfully,

The Real Life Community Church Board
Mary Beth Hanson, Michael Whiting, Julianna Poe, Michael Vernor, Cheryl Oord

1

2

3

4 THIS SPACE INTENTIONALLY LEFT BLANK

5

6

7

8 --

9

10 JUD-811a

11

12 DISCIPLINE OF A MEMBER OF THE CLERGY

13 Southwest Indiana District, Virginia District General

14 Assembly Delegates

15 Manual 606.1

16

17

18 RESOLVED that Manual paragraph 606.1 be amended as

19 follows:

20

21 606.1. If a member of the clergy is accused of conduct

22 unbecoming a minister or of teaching doctrines out of

23 harmony with the [doctrinal statement] Articles of Faith,

24 the Agreed Statement of Belief, The Covenant of Christian

25 Character, and The Covenant of Christian Conduct of the

26 Church of the Nazarene such accusations shall be placed in

27 writing and shall be signed by at least two members of the

28 Church of the Nazarene who are at the time in good

29 standing. Accusations of sexual misconduct cannot be

30 signed by any person who consented to participate in the

JUD-811a English /page 2
1 alleged misconduct. The written accusation must be filed

2 with the district superintendent who shall present it to the

3 District Advisory Board of the district where the accused has

4 ministerial membership. This accusation shall become part

5 of the record in the case.

6 The District Advisory Board shall give written notice to

7 the accused that accusations have been filed, as soon as

8 practical by any method which gives actual notice. When

9 actual notice is not practical, notice may be provided in the

10 manner which is customary for serving legal notices in that

11 locality. The accused and his or her counsel shall have the

12 right to examine the accusations and to receive a written

13 copy of the same immediately upon request. (540.4, 540.9,

14 540.12)

15

16

17 REASONS:

18

19 1. It is unclear as to what constitutes the "doctrinal
20 statements" of the Church of the Nazarene.

21

22 2. Different districts have identified the "doctrinal
23 statement" of the Church of the Nazarene in different
24 ways so that one district may uphold a charge as being
25 out of harmony with the doctrinal statement, while
26 another district may dismiss the same charge, denying
27 that it is a matter of doctrine.

28

29 3. This resolution helps remove the subjectivity of
30 identifying what is and what is not a part of the
"doctrinal

JUD-811a English /page 3
1 statements."

WHY THE CHURCH OF THE

NAZARENE

SHOULD BE FULLY

LGBTQ+

AFFIRMING

THOMAS JAY OORD and ALEXA OORD, editors

PREFACE TO
WHY THE CHURCH OF THE NAZARENE SHOULD BE FULLY LGBTQ+ AFFIRMING

The essays in this book were written in response to an invitation. We (Tom and Alexa) invited people to contribute to a book we would title, "Why the Church of the Nazarene Should be Fully LGBTQ+ Affirming." You're reading that book.

Despite the shared theme, the essays published here are diverse. Some are written by Queer people, and they narrate portions of their life journeys. Those narratives often include struggles and the eventual affirmation of their LGBTQ+ identities and experiences as healthy rather than sinful. Many felt persecuted by people and the culture of the Church of the Nazarene, so they left the denomination. They did not feel loved. Other Queer people remain but feel marginalized, shamed, and traumatized.

Some essay writers are parents, siblings, or allies of LGBTQ+ people. Most who become fully affirming do so because of close relationships with Queer loved ones.

Some parents, for instance, felt compelled to rethink their views on LGBTQ+ matters after their children "came out" or identified as non-heteronormative. Many reevaluated what it means to live as healthy people in healthy societies. They now believe God loves and affirms Queer people.

Some contributors to this book are pastors, scholars, or leaders in the church. They believe the denomination needs to change its views on human sexuality and the way it treats those who support Queer people. Some of these writers call for honest conversations, including impunity for those who think current Manual statements fail to reflect well the love of Jesus.[1] In other essays, scholars explain why scripture, theology, and history support a fully affirming LGBTQ+ position.

By "fully affirming," contributors *don't* mean "anything goes" sexually. After all, "not everything is beneficial," to quote the Apostle Paul (1 Cor. 10:23). Some sexual activity—homosexual and heterosexual—isn't healthy, and life-long partnerships in marriage have immense value. They mean they fully affirm people with LGBTQ+ identities, orientations, and desires. The denomination's current statement on human sexuality does not reflect well the love Jesus calls his followers to express.

Although this book has more than 90 contributors, one may think a tiny percentage of Nazarenes want change.

---

1. The call for safe and irenic discussion of LGBTQ issues is also present among Church of the Nazarene clergy. See the doctoral work of Reg Watson on this matter (R. G. Watson, *Nazarene Clergy Responses to Homosexuality and Interactions with LGBT People* [Doctoral dissertation, Regent University, 2015]). See also Bruce Barnard's research and preliminary writing in preparation for dissertation work, "You're Losing Us - The LGBTQ Community and the Church of the Nazarene."

But there are good reasons to believe hundreds of thousands in the denomination agree with the book's contributors, and that number rises daily. A 2007 Pew poll showed that 31% of Americans who identify with the Church of the Nazarene thought society should accept homosexuality. That percentage jumped to 40% by 2014.[2] We suspect the percentage is higher today.

A Barna Report indicates that 46% of Christians under the age of 40 want laws to protect Same-Sex Marriage and LGBTQ+ rights.[3] Two major takeaways from that Barna survey are 1) American Christians increasingly accept LGBTQ+ people and their healthy sexual behavior, and 2) younger American Christians are more accepting of Queer people than older Americans.

Young people are leaving the Church of the Nazarene. Many believe the denomination's views on human sexuality do not reflect the love of God. A 2008 poll of twenty religious groups said the holiness tradition—of which the Church of the Nazarene is the largest denomination—is the *worst* of all religious groups at retaining their young people. Only 32% of Nazarene youth remain.[4] A similar poll in 2015 showed no change in this rate of exit.[5]

---

2. See https://www.pewresearch.org/fact-tank/2015/12/18/most-u-s-christian-groups-grow-more-accepting-of-homosexuality/

3. See https://www.barna.com/research/americas-change-of-mind-on-same-sex-marriage-and-lgbtq-rights/

4. See http://thomasjayoord.com/index.php/blog/archives/atheists_only_slightly_worse_at_retaining_children_than_holiness_folk

5. See https://www.pewforum.org/2015/05/12/chapter-2-religious-switching-and-intermarriage/pr_15-05-12_rls_chapter2-04/

The Church of the Nazarene is global, of course, and while the USA segment is the strongest financially, it represents a fairly small in membership percentage overall. Our experience among European Nazarenes, however, is that the majority are more progressive on LGBTQ+ issues than American Nazarenes. But African and Latin-American Nazarenes are less progressive on this issue, and less progressive on other issues, such as women in leadership and modesty in dress.

These essays also tell a story. It's a narrative about how a marginalized group has been mistreated and denied full acceptance. That story points to a loving and accepting God who calls us all to love and accept Queer people. A peculiarly loving God loves peculiar people of all varieties and wants us to do the same. This love means full acceptance of LGBTQ+ people, their identities, orientations, and healthy sexual expressions.

As editors, we hope these essays foster that acceptance. We believe the Church of the Nazarene has something positive to offer the world. But the heart of the denomination's message—love—has been muted and muffled by its statements about LGBTQ+ people.

In the spirit of spurring "one another to love and good deeds," as the writer of Hebrews puts it (10:24), we offer this book.

THOMAS JAY OORD and ALEXA OORD

(This blog essay was first posted in June of 2023 on lovingnazarenes.com.)

DISINGENUOUS

That's the most charitable word to describe your actions in recent days. Disingenuous. The actions to which I am referring are characterized by quotes like the following:

In your (Caleb's) review of *Why the Church of the Nazarene Should be Fully LGBTQ+ Affirming*, you say, "First, we should call Nazarenes who reject the denomination's stance on human sexuality to repent—including Thomas Oord and other Nazarene authors in this book. Second, we should remove the credentials of Nazarene clergy who refuse to repent—including Thomas Oord and the sixteen other authors in the book who are ordained Nazarene ministers. Similarly, we should relieve any LGBTQ+ affirming faculty at Nazarene institutions of their positions and titles."

In your (Jared's) blog, you claim, "More evidence is readily available for Oord to lose his credential in the Church of the Nazarene." And near the end, you ask what seems to be a rhetorical question, "Why does Oord still have his credentials?"

Your (Matt and Elijah's) edited book is a response "to members of the Nazarene tribe [who] have sought to amplify their opinions regarding sex and gender issues...," an apparent reference to *Why the Church of the Nazarene Should be Fully LGBTQ+ Affirming.* Some essayists in the book say people like me should be disciplined for wanting changes on the denomination's statement on human sexuality.

Biblical Inerrancy

To understand my claim that you're disingenuous, we need to return to 2009. In that year, a proposal from the Southwest Indiana District came to General Assembly. It asked for radical change to the denomination's Article on Scripture.

The proposal sought to remove the phrase "inerrantly revealing the will of God concerning us in all things necessary to our salvation." The replacement said the Bible is "inerrant throughout, and the supreme authority on everything the Scriptures teach."

Correct me if I'm wrong, but I believe some people now in the Holiness Partnership advocated for this change. And many in the Partnership today would like to see something similar replace the Manual's current statement on

Scripture. (See Concerned Nazarene and Former Nazarene statements.)

The General Assembly committee sent the Southwest Indiana proposal to what it called a "Scripture Study Committee." That group subsequently issued a document they called, "Report of the Scripture Study Committee." (Find the full report here.)

The committee strongly supported the denomination's longstanding statement on Scripture. They did not want an Article of Faith that said the Bible was "inerrant throughout." The committee believed the proposed change had a "Calvinist origin" and reflected "Calvinist belief."

In other words, the proposed changes did not fit a Wesleyan-Holiness view of the Bible.

STAN REEDER

During this time, I was in conversation with Stan Reeder, who was then the district superintendent of the Oregon-Pacific District. He's now USA/Canada regional director. The recent statement claiming all major sections of the Manual are essential came from his office.

Stan interpreted Article 4 as saying something similar to what the Southwest Indiana district had proposed. In my discussions with Stan, I said those changes assume a Calvinist view of biblical inspiration. They did not reflect our theological commitments.

Of course, the Scripture committee eventually sided with my perspective. I did not respond, however, by asking Stan to leave the denomination. Nor did I seek to have him disciplined. And to my knowledge, no one from the Southwest Indiana district was asked to leave when their changes were not adopted by the General Assembly. They were not disciplined.

Inerrant in Autographs

Now, to my primary point...

You (Matt and Elijah Friedeman) are employed by Wesley Biblical Seminary (Mississippi). And you (Jared Henry) are a trustee at Kentucky Mountain Bible College. But these two institutions have statements on the Bible that do not align with the Church of the Nazarene's Article on Scripture.

Both institutions claim the original documents of the Bible are inerrant. That's not what we find in the Church of the Nazarene's Manual. The idea that the original biblical autographs are inerrant is not only unverifiable. It's the kind of claim you'll find in Calvinist-oriented institutions like Wheaton.

In other words, the people wanting to discipline me and others are out of step with the Manual's statement on Scripture!

It could be, of course, that you (the Friedemans and Henry) are actively trying to change the Scripture statements at the institutions at which you serve. But if you are, you're being disingenuous when you seek change but don't allow others to do the same.

More likely, however, you (the Friedemans and Henry) endorse the original autograph inerrancy views of Wesley

Biblical Seminary and Kentucky Mountain Bible College. You embrace them, even though they diverge from the Manual. And yet you want to discipline me and others who want changes in the Manual.

Disingenuous.

THE LETTER KILLS

I'm not surprised that you (the Friedemans and Henry) have views that don't fit the Manual of the Church of the Nazarene. We Nazarenes are a diverse bunch! Any independent-thinking person is bound to come to conclusions that don't fit the Manual perfectly.

I do not plan to ask for you to be disciplined, however. I will turn the other cheek. Love does not repay evil with evil.

I fear, however, that your call to remove my credentials returns the denomination to the Fundamentalist legalism of yesteryear. As someone who grew up seeing such legalism, I had hoped the denomination had matured. Afterall, living by the letter of the Manual kills.

My hope is that we have a real conversation without calling for credentials and without seeking discipline. Let's come to the table in good faith. And rather than saber rattling, let's hear our differences on Scripture, science, culture, and more.

Let's aim for genuine love (Rom. 12:9).

BIBLIOGRAPHIES

COMPILED BY KEEGAN OSINSKI...

Brawley, Robert L. *Biblical Ethics & Homosexuality: Listening to Scripture*. 1st ed. Louisville, Ky: Westminster John Knox Press, 1996.

Brownson, James V. *Bible, Gender, Sexuality: Reframing the Church's Debate on Same-Sex Relationships*. Grand Rapids, Mich: Eerdmans, 2013.

Cheng, Patrick S. *Radical Love: An Introduction to Queer Theology*. 1 edition. Seabury, 2011.

———. *Rainbow Theology: Bridging Race, Sexuality, and Spirit*. New York: Seabury, 2013.

Conley, Garrard. *Boy Erased: A Memoir of Identity, Faith, and Family*. Reprint edition. New York: Riverhead Books, 2017.

Coogan, Michael. *God and Sex: What the Bible Really Says*. Reprint edition. New York; London: Twelve, 2011.

Cornwall, Susannah. *Sex and Uncertainty in the Body of Christ: Intersex Conditions and Christian Theology*. Gender, Theology and Spirituality. London ; Equinox, 2010.

DeFranza, Megan K. *Sex Difference in Christian Theology: Male, Female, and Intersex in the Image of God*. Eerdmans, 2015.

DiNovo, Cheri. *Qu(e)Erying Evangelism: Growing a Community from the Outside In*. Center for Lesbian and Gay Studies in Religion and Ministry. Cleveland, Ohio: Pilgrim Press, 2005.

Douglas, Kelly B. *Sexuality and the Black Church: A Womanist Perspective*. Maryknoll, N.Y: Orbis Books, 1999.

Ellison, Marvin M., and Kelly Brown Douglas, eds. *Sexuality and the Sacred, Second Edition: Sources for Theological Reflection*. 2nd edition. Louisville, Ky: Westminster John Knox, 2010.

Farley, Margaret. *Just Love: Framework for Christian Sexual Ethics*. London: Continuum, 2008.

Fausto-Sterling, Anne. *Sex/Gender: Biology in a Social World*. New York: Routledge, 2012.

Goss, Robert E., and Mona West. *Take Back the Word: A Queer Reading of the Bible*. Cleveland, Ohio: The Pilgrim Press, 2000.

Guest, Deryn, Robert Goss, and Mona West, eds. *The Queer Bible Commentary*. SCM, 2015.

Gushee, David P. *Changing Our Mind: Definitive 3rd Edition of the Landmark Call for Inclusion of LGBTQ Christians with Response to Critics*. 3 edition. Read the Spirit Books, 2017.

Steve Harper, *Holy Love: A Biblical Theology of Human Sexuality*. Nashville: Abingdon, 2019.

Harrison, Nonna Verna. *God's Many-Splendored Image: Theological Anthropology for Christian Formation*. 59250th edition. Grand Rapids, Mich: Baker Academic, 2010.

Hartke, Austen. *Transforming: The Bible and the Lives of Transgender Christians*. Louisville, KY: Westminster John Knox Press, 2018.

Himbaza, Innocent. *The Bible on the Question of Homosexuality*. Washington, D.C: Catholic University of America Press, 2012.

Hornsby, Teresa J., and Deryn Guest. *Transgender, Intersex, and Biblical Interpretation*. Semeia Studies ; Number 83. Atlanta: SBL Press, 2016.

Isherwood, Lisa. *The Power of Erotic Celibacy: Queering Heteropatriarchy*. Queering Theology Series. London ; T & T Clark, 2006.

Jakobsen, Janet, and Ann Pellegrini. *Love the Sin: Sexual Regulation and the Limits of Religious Tolerance*. Boston, Mass.: Beacon Press, 2004.

Jordan, Mark. *The Ethics of Sex*. 1 edition. Oxford, UK ; Malden, Mass: Wiley-Blackwell, 2002.

Jordan, Mark D. *The Invention of Sodomy in Christian Theology*. The Chicago Series on Sexuality, History, and Society. Chicago, IL: University of Chicago Press, 1998. https://press.uchicago.edu/ucp/books/book/chicago/I/bo3644992.html.

Kim-Kort, Mihee. *Outside the Lines: How Embracing Queerness Will Transform Your Faith*. Minneapolis, MN: Fortress Press, 2018.

Knust, Jennifer. *Abandoned to Lust: Sexual Slander and Ancient Christianity*. New York: Columbia University Press, 2005.

Lee, Justin. *Torn: Rescuing the Gospel from the Gays-vs.-Christians Debate*. Jericho, 2012.

Lightsey, Pamela R. *Our Lives Matter: A Womanist Queer Theology*. Eugene, Oregon: Pickwick Publications, 2015.

Loughlin, Gerard, ed. *Queer Theology: Rethinking the Western Body*. Malden, MA ; Blackwell Pub, 2007.

Martin, Colby. *Unclobber: Rethinking Our Misuse of the Bible on Homosexuality*. First edition. Louisville, Kentucky: Westminster John Knox Press, 2016.

Michaelson, Jay. *God vs. Gay?: The Religious Case for Equality*. Queer Action/Queer Ideas. Boston: Beacon Press, 2011.

Mollenkott, Virginia Ramey, and Letha Dawson Scanzoni. *Is the Homosexual My Neighbor? Revised and Updated: Positive Christian Response, A*. San Francisco, Calif.: HarperOne, 1994.

Moon, Dawne. *God, Sex, and Politics: Homosexuality and Everyday Theologies*. Chicago: University of Chicago Press, 2004.

Rogers, Jack. *Jesus, the Bible, and Homosexuality: Explode the Myths, Heal the Church*. 1st ed. Louisville, Ky: Westminster John Knox Press, 2006.

Schlager, Bernard, and David Kundtz. *Ministry Among God's Queer Folk, Second Edition: LGBTQ Pastoral Care*. Cascade Books, an Imprint of Wipf and Stock Publishers, 2019.

Shore-Goss, Robert Everett, Thomas Bohache, Patrick S. Cheng, and Ramona Faye West. *Queering Christianity: Finding a Place at the Table for LGBTQI Christians*. Santa Barbara, California: Praeger, 2013.

Soughers, Tara K. *Beyond a Binary God: A Theology for Trans* Allies*. Church, 2018.

Stone, Ken. *Queer Commentary and the Hebrew Bible*. 1st edition. London ; New York: Sheffield Academic Press, 2002.

Tonstad, Linn Marie. *Queer Theology: Beyond Apologetics*. Eugene, Oregon: Cascade, 2018.

Vines, Matthew. *God and the Gay Christian: The Biblical Case in Support of Same-Sex Relationships*. Convergent Books, 2014.

White, Mel. *Stranger at the Gate: To Be Gay and Christian in America*. Reprint edition. New York: Plume, 1995.

Wilcox, Melissa M. *Coming Out in Christianity: Religion, Identity, and Community.* First Edition. Bloomington: Indiana University Press, 2003.

Wold, Donald J. *Out of Order: Homosexuality in the Bible and the Ancient Near East.* Grand Rapids, Mich: Baker Books, 1998.

Doctoral Dissertations about and/or by Nazarenes on Queer Issues

Bruce Barnard, "Cognitive Dissonance and the Progression of the Church on Major Cultural Norms," (D.Min., George Fox University, 2016).

Michael Joseph Brennan, "Open and Relational Queer Theology: A Catalyst for Queer Affirmation through a Comparative Analysis of Sovereignty and Love," (Doctoral dissertation, Northwind Theological Seminary, in progress).

Jacob Gilbertson, "Creating support for students who identify as lesbian, gay, bisexual, transgender, queer, or questioning (LGBTQ) at an evangelical university: An action research study" (Doctoral dissertation, Azusa Pacific University, 2019).

Kimberly A. Purl, "Disinherited: Former Ministry Students in the Church of the Nazarene," (D.Min. Eden Theological Seminary, 2023).

Reginald G. Watson, 'Nazarene Clergy Responses to
    Homosexuality and Interactions with LGBT People,"
    (Doctoral dissertation, Regent University, 2015).

Special Consideration

Jonathan Foster, *Questions about Sexuality that Got Me
    Uninvited from My Denomination* (Verde Group, 2019).

Resources Compiled by Erin Moorman...

LGBTQI2A+ Affirming Faith

* **Bible Trouble: Queer Reading at the Boundaries of
  Biblical Scholarship** | K. Stone, T.J. Hornsby

* **Filled with the Spirit: Sexuality, Gender, and Radical
  Inclusivity in a Black Pentecostal Church Coalition** |
  Ellen Lewin

* **For I Am Wonderfully Made: Texts on Eastern
  Orthodoxy and LGBT Inclusion** | M. Cherniak,
  O. Gerassimenko, M. Brinkschröder, eds.

* **God and the Gay Christian** | Matthew Vines

* **Included in Christ: Scripturally Unraveling the
  Apparent Incongruity Between Gay Christians and the
  Church's Belief in "One Man, One Woman"** | Cristy
  Perdue MD

* **Oriented to Faith** | Tim Otto

- **Our Strangely Warmed Hearts: Coming Out into Gods Call** | Karen P. Oliveto

- **Outside the Lines: How Embracing Queerness Will Transform Your Faith** | Mihee Kim-Kort

- **Queer Virtue: What LGBTQ People Know About Life and Love and How It Can Revitalize Christianity** | The Rev Elizabeth M. Edman

- **Queerfully and Wonderfully Made: A Guide for LGBTQ+ Christian Teens** | Leigh Finke

- **Queering Christianity: Finding a Place at the Table for LGBTQI Christians** | R. Shore-Goss, T. Bohache, P. Cheng, M. West, eds.

- **Queering Wesley, Queering the Church** | Keegan Osinski

- **Radical Love: An Introduction to Queer Theology** | Patrick Cheng

- **Rainbow Theology: Bridging Race, Sexuality, and Spirit** | Patrick Cheng

- **Rescuing Jesus: How People of Color, Women, and Queer Christians are Reclaiming Evangelicalism** | Deborah Jian Lee

- **Take Back the Word: A Queer Reading of the Bible** | Robert E. Goss

- **The Gospel of Inclusion, Revised Edition: A Christian Case for LGBT+ Inclusion in the Church** | Brandan J. Robertson, David P. Gushee

- **Torn** | Justin Lee

- **Us Versus Us: The Untold Story of Religion and the LGBT Community** | Andrew Marin

- **Walking the Bridgeless Canyon: Repairing the Breach between the Church and the LGBT community** | Kathy Baldock

- **Wrestling with God and Men: Homosexuality in the Jewish Tradition** | Steven Greenberg

Trans & Intersex Affirming Faith

- **In the Margins: A Transgender Man's Journey with Scripture** | Shannon T. L. Kearns

- **Sex and Uncertainty in the Body of Christ: Intersex Conditions and Christian Theology** | Susannah Cornwall

- **Sex Difference in Christian Theology: Male, Female, and Intersex in the Image of God** | Megan K. DeFranza

- **The Bible and the Transgender Experience: How Scripture Supports Gender Variance** | Linda Herzer

- **This is My Body: Hearing the Theology of Transgender Christians** | Christina Beardsley

- **Transforming: The Bible and the Lives of Transgender Christians** | Austin Hartke

- **Trans-Gender: Theology, Ministry, and Communities of Faith** | Justin Sabia-Tanis

- **Transgender, Intersex, and Biblical Interpretation** | Teresa J. Hornsby

For Allies

- **Beyond a Binary God: A Theology for Trans Allies** | Tara K. Soughers

- **Made, Known, Loved: Developing LGBTQ-Inclusive Youth Ministry** | Ross Murray

- **"Mom, I'm Gay": Loving Your LGBTQ Child and Strengthening Your Faith** | Susan Cottrell, Justin Lee

- **Supporting Trans People of Colour: How to Make Your Practice Inclusive** | Sabah Choudrey

- **Trans Affirming Churches: How to Celebrate Gender-Variant People and Their Loved Ones** | C. Beardsley, C. Dowd

Websites & Organizations

- **CenterPeace** (https://www.centerpeace.net/)

- **DignityUSA** (https://www.dignityusa.org/)

- **Enfleshed**—*Expansive, affirming, anti-racist liturgical resources*(https://enfleshed.com/)

- **Many Voices**—*A Black Church Movement for Gay & Transgender Justice*

- (www.manyvoices.org/)

- **Loving Nazarenes** (https://lovingnazarenes.com)

- **Oriented To Love** (https://christiansforsocialaction.org/programs/oriented-to-love/)

- **Q Christian Fellowship**—*Resources and community for LGBTQI2A Christians*

- (https://www.qchristian.org/)

- **Queer Grace**—*An LGBTQI2A faith encyclopedia* (www.queergrace.com/)

- **Queer Theology**—*Resources and community for LGBTQI2A Christians* (www.queertheology.com/)

- **Reconciling Ministries Network** (https://rmnetwork.org/)

- **Reformation Project** (https://reformationproject.org/)

- **Room for All** (https://roomforall.com/)

- **Roots and Branches Network** (https://www.rootsandbranchesnetwork.com/)

- **The Center for LGBTQ and Gender Studies in Religion** (https://clgs.org/)

- **TransFaith**—*Information and community for LGBTQI2A people of all faiths*

- (www.transfaith.info/)

- **Transmission Ministry Collective**—*Online resources and community for trans and gender-expansive Christians* (www.transmissionministry.com/)

- **The 6 Most Common Biological Sexes in Humans** (https://www.joshuakennon.com/the-six-commo n-biological-sexes-in-humans/)

Thomas Jay Oord, Ph.D., is a theologian, philosopher, and scholar of multi-disciplinary studies. Oord directs the Center for Open and Relational Theology and doctoral students at Northwind Theological Seminary. He is an award-winning author and has written or edited more than thirty books. A gifted speaker, Oord lectures at universities, conferences, churches, and institutions. He is known for his contributions to research on love, science and religion, open and relational theology, the problem of suffering, and the implications of freedom for transformational relationships. For more on Oord, see his website: thomasjayoord.com

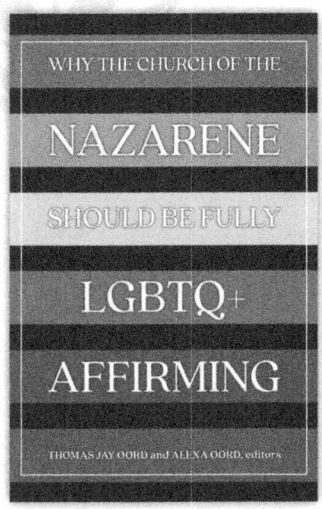

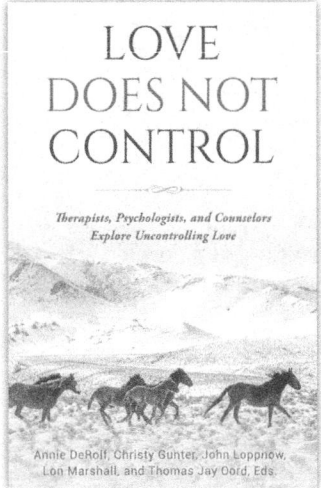

Made in the USA
Las Vegas, NV
19 June 2024

91236103R00066